TWAYNE'S WORLD AUTHORS SERIES

A Survey of the World's Literature

FRANCE

Maxwell A. Smith, Guerry Professor of French, Emeritus
The University of Chattanooga
Former Visiting Professor in Modern Languages
The Florida State University

EDITOR

Jean Giraudoux

TWAS 513

Jean Giraudoux

JEAN GIRAUDOUX

By JOHN H. REILLY

*Queens College of the
City University of New York*

TWAYNE PUBLISHERS

A DIVISION OF G. K. HALL & CO., BOSTON

Published in 1978 by Twayne Publishers,
A Division of G. K. Hall & Co.
All Rights Reserved

Printed on permanent/ durable acid-free paper and bound
in the United States of America

First Printing

Library of Congress Cataloging in Publication Data

Reilly, John H.
Jean Giraudoux.

(Twayne's world authors series ; TWAS 513 : France)
Bibliography: p. 159–63
Includes index.
1. Giraudoux, Jean, 1882–1944.
2. Authors, French—20th century—Biography.
PQ2613.I74Z784   848'.9'1209   78-19156
ISBN 0-8057-6354-6

Contents

About the Author

John H. Reilly received his B.A. degree from Syracuse University and the M.A. and Ph.D. degrees from the University of Wisconsin. He has taught at the latter institution and at Bowling Green State University and is currently Associate Professor of Romance Languages at Queens College of the City University of New York. Professor Reilly has previously published a book on Arthur Adamov for the Twayne Series as well as a text edition of Jean Giraudoux's *Intermezzo.* In addition, he has published articles in the *French Review* and is the American contributor to the bibliography of the *Revue d'Histoire du Théâtre.* His fields of interest include the contemporary French theater as well as contemporary European and American theater.

Preface

Since he first began writing in 1909, Jean Giraudoux's work has received a variety of critical interpretations attesting to its complexity and its richness. In his first published stories, he was seen as a stylist, a magician with words, a *fantaisiste.* At the same time, many of the early critics thought of him as light and superficial, a *précieux,* someone with an exaggerated, somewhat affected manner. After the publication of several novels, Giraudoux was considered an original writer, but he did not have wide support from reviewers or the public. In 1928, however, when his play *Siegfried* was presented, he emerged from the ranks of the minor novelists and scored a stunning theatrical success. Even then, though, he was thought to be too removed from reality to have anything of much importance to say. Finally, in 1935, the first performance of *Tiger at the Gates* marked him as a writer who dealt with serious topics and deserved consideration. The play treated the subject of the inevitability of war and touched upon a nerve in the French people of that time. His later works, which became more and more pessimistic about the human condition, confirmed that Giraudoux was an author oftentimes of tragic proportions.

In 1940, Jean-Paul Sartre, the distinguished philosopher and writer, presented a penetrating essay on the Aristotelianism of Giraudoux, providing new insight into his work. After World War II, critics continued to discover the depth and variety of Giraudoux's writings. Some probed his attitude toward language and analyzed his universe in terms of rhetoric and metaphor. Others saw that, far from being simply witty and amusing, Giraudoux had a very definite concept of man and of his role in the universe. René Marill Albérès's major work, *Esthétique et morale chez Jean Giraudoux* (1957), argues convincingly that Giraudoux sensed a tragic discord between man and the universe and that he tried to achieve a harmony or equilibrium between the real world in which man lives and the cosmos that he seeks. Recent studies have looked at the writer from new perspectives. Agnès Raymond sees Giraudoux as a political author to a much greater extent than had previously been imagined. Charles Mauron presents a psychocritical study of the man, pointing out how the writer's work reflects a conflict between his inner and outer selves. Most recently (1975), Jacques Body has published a highly impressive study on Giraudoux and Germany in which he details the influence of Germany — its spirit and its literature — upon Giraudoux's creative processes.

Over the years it has become increasingly clear that Giraudoux's writings are not dilettantish and escapist but rather are an expression of and a reaction to the reality that surrounded him. The writer, who had often been criticized for having nothing to say about the real world, was actually constantly responding to reality, and his works took their direction from it. Far from being will-o'-the-wisp, his literary efforts convey his deepest personal preoccupations. From his earliest years as a child, he had developed a certain detachment and aloofness from what seemed to him an imperfect reality. As the years passed and he began writing, he soon discovered the one essential goal in his life and the major theme in his novels and plays: How can man go beyond his immediate reality? How can he transcend his everyday, drab existence? How can he find the ideal? In his writing from 1909 through 1944, Giraudoux asked these questions in a variety of ways and through several seemingly diverse topics. However, his work does follow a certain progression and can be separated into three major periods: 1909–1920; 1921–1934; and 1935–1944.

Although these divisions are somewhat arbitrary, they nonetheless offer a fairly accurate picture of Giraudoux's evolution as a writer and provide a framework around which to develop our discussion. During his first period (1909–1920), Giraudoux's works were mainly autobiographical. At the beginning, they were drawn from his experiences as a child in the Limousin area, then as a young man in Paris and later as a soldier in World War I. In all of these writings, he has not yet found his basic theme, but he has learned to transcend reality with his style. His unique points of view, his whimsy, his inventive and creative juxtaposition of words create a world that is highly original and distinctive. His characters are part of reality, but the writer has already begun his efforts to transcend it.

The second period (1921–1934) is the time of his most typical writing and the moment when his theme of the conflict of the real and the ideal is presented in its most basic form. In works like

Preface

Suzanne and the Pacific or *Intermezzo,* Giraudoux uses the young girl as his protagonist, the *jeune fille* in her adolescence, seeking the unknown, the realm of adventure, the escape from an unchanging reality. Inevitably, her pursuit of the ideal fails, and the girl must return to the real world to learn to develop her imagination within it. At this point, Giraudoux is looking outward toward the cosmos and nature, searching for a union between man (reality) and the universe (the ideal). However, in the latter part of this period, some signs of discontent appear. He becomes more pessimistic, and the possibility of finding a harmony between the ideal and the real begins to seem remote.

In the third and last period (1935–1944), the pessimism increases, and there is little likelihood of harmony. Reality, which the author sought to overcome all his life, has become all too present, and he can no longer escape it: he now faces the difficulties of middle age, his marriage begins to experience considerable strain, and a new war is on the verge of erupting between France and Germany. All of this symbolizes the end of his dreams. *Tiger at the Gates* probably represents the turning point in his writing, as Giraudoux realizes that the world is made up of forces that man cannot control and that the unknown, rather than being an ideal or goal, has become a hostile presence. As a result, he turns away from the cosmos as a means of coping with reality and turns instead to face the real world. His themes now become more human—war, the couple, love, politics, urbanism. However, even now, all of these topics grow out of the imperfections that he sees in his life and that he seeks to improve, a goal that he cannot achieve.

In this study, I have presented a literary analysis of Giraudoux's novels and plays using the chronological divisions given above as guidelines. In general, I have not included any discussion of his essays because of space limitations. All the quotations from the writings are in English, and the translations are my own. The quotations from the novels and plays are taken (with only occasional exceptions) from the works of Giraudoux published by Grasset between 1954 and 1958. Each edition is first identified in a note, and all subsequent citations are incorporated into the text of the study. A selective bibliography has been included at the end of the study, listing those works that were particularly useful in the preparation of this book. Many important books or articles from the extensive Giraudoux bibliography have not been included since they were less applicable to the points discussed in this study.

Chronology

1924   Publication of *Juliette au pays des hommes*. Involvement in dispute of Philippe Berthelot and Raymond Poincaré. Sent briefly to embassy in Germany.

1925   Treaty of Locarno.

1926   Publication of *Bella*. Meets director and actor Louis Jouvet.

1927   Named to Commission on the Assessment of Allied Damages in Turkey. Publication of *Eglantine*.

1928   May 3: Presentation of first play, *Siegfried*. Briand-Kellogg peace pact.

1929   November 9: *Amphitryon 38*.

1930   Publication of essay, "Racine." Publication of *Aventures de Jérôme Bardini*.

1931   November 4: *Judith*.

1932   Publication of *La France sentimentale*.

1933   February 27: *Intermezzo*. Rise to power of Hitler.

1934   November 14: *Tessa*. Publication of *Combat avec l'ange*. Named inspector general of Diplomatic and Consular Posts Abroad.

1935   November 21: *La Guerre de Troie n'aura pas lieu* and *Supplément au voyage de Cook*.

1937   May 13: *Electre*. December 4: *L'Impromptu de Paris*.

1938   October 12: *Cantique des cantiques*. Publication of *Les Cinq Tentations de la Fontaine*.

1939   April 27: *Ondine*. Publication of *Choix des élues* and *Pleins Pouvoirs*. Beginning of World War II. Named to head office of French wartime propaganda.

1940   Invasion and defeat of France. Retires to family home at Cussett, near Vichy.

1941   Publication of *Littérature*.

1942   Returns to Paris. June 10: *L'Apollon de Bellac,* first presented by Jouvet in Rio de Janeiro. Publication of film script, *La Duchesse de Langeais*.

1943   October 11: *Sodome et Gomorrhe*. Death of Giraudoux's ninety year old mother.

1944   January 31: Death of Giraudoux in Paris. Liberation of Paris from German occupation. Publication of film script *Les Anges du péché*.

1945   December 19: *La Folle de Chaillot*.

1946   Publication of *Sans pouvoirs*.

1947   April 19: *L'Apollon de Bellac,* first performance in France. Publication of *Visitations*.

Chronology

CHAPTER 1

The Development of a Writer

I The Years of Schooling

AS a major writer, Jean Giraudoux spent a great deal of his time
in Paris, one of the capitals of the world. Later, his work in the
diplomatic circles of government took him to other important cities
throughout the globe. However, no matter where he traveled and
no matter what new experiences he encountered, he always retained
a special affection for the small towns of provincial France.

Hippolyte Jean Giraudoux was born on October 29, 1882, in
Bellac, a rural hamlet in the Haute-Vienne region in the old province of Limousin. In his works, especially in his novels, the writer
bestowed lavish praise on the beauties and the quaint charms of his
native town and of the Limousin area. In a speech in 1928, he spoke
of this region with particular pleasure, calling it "a country of
plains which do not attempt to be imposing, of discreet country-
sides, of brooks which do not attempt to babble"[1] — that is, a
place of harmony and tranquillity. Giraudoux knew the area well,
as his father moved about a great deal in the boy's younger years.
Léger Giraudoux worked in the department of highways in Bellac.
However, when Jean was seven, his father moved to Bessines, seeking a better climate for his arthritis. Later, the family went to Pelle-
voisin, where the father was a tax collector, then to Cérilly and to
Cusset in the same region. Giraudoux's father was an ordinary civil
servant who performed his work conscientiously. However, he was
a taciturn, uncommunicative man, and Jean was never very close to
him. On the other hand, he was extremely devoted to his mother,
Anne, and this devotion lasted throughout his lifetime as she died
only two months before he did. A pleasant but reserved woman,
she had a dislike for any unusual familiarity on the part of people,
a sentiment that her son also shared. Refined and discreet, she also

passed on other traits to her son: "An innate elegance, which was also a defense mechanism, a tendency to live in a world slightly superior to that around her without, however, separating herself from reality."[2] Giraudoux's brother, Alexandre, was two years older, and although apparently very dissimilar, they had a close relationship during their lifetime. Alexandre, who later became a doctor, was a practical person, Jean was less earthbound, more detached.[3]

From 1893 to 1900, Giraudoux attended the lycée of Châteauroux on a scholarship. A bright student, he was a bit distant from his classmates, most of whom were much less refined. He applied himself to his studies and received particularly good training in Latin and Greek. This early acquaintance with the classics excited the future writer, and he was to remember and use some of this learning later in his novels and plays. The strict intellectual discipline of the time and the strongly rationalistic method of reasoning had a marked influence on the early Giraudoux. Another important influence was also at work. Like the majority of French schoolboys of this period, he studied German, and for Giraudoux, this was an imaginative and strange new world that he was only beginning to explore. Even in these early years at Châteauroux, he had a keen ear for the beauties of language in general, caring little or not at all for slang. He especially enjoyed writing compositions for his classes, and the idea of a literary career must have already been in his mind, for he wrote to several authors requesting advice.[4] He also displayed some early interest in the theater, and he and his cousins used to present plays for their own amusement: "In my childhood, I used to spend my vacations from the pension in a family of numerous cousins and we entertained ourselves each month on Sundays by presenting ... a play directed by an elderly cousin who was a Capuchin friar."[5]

In October 1900, Giraudoux entered the Lycée Lakanal in Paris, where he planned to prepare for the entrance examination to the Ecole Normale Supérieure.[6] In the beginning, at least, he remained the same in personality and character as he had been earlier: a diligent student; friendly to others but slightly distant; smiling, but possessing perhaps a trace of mischief. He continued his work in Latin and Greek, but interrupted his study of German for two years.[7] Although he failed on his first attempt, he eventually was admitted to the Ecole Normale. Before entering, though, he completed his military service in 1902–1903 and, shortly thereafter, was given the rank of reserve sergeant.

His admission to the Ecole Normale was an important moment for Giraudoux, for he was now confronted with other equally or more intelligent students who were carefully selected and who would go on later to assume important positions in government, education, business, and literature. At this stage, the students had an imaginative, ideal approach to life, coupled with a definite penchant for irony and a rather fanciful humor, qualities that fit Giraudoux perfectly: "He remained until the end of his life an idealist, although he never rid himself of a certain intellectual flippancy, an inordinate love for verbal acrobatics, and a persistent fondness of spoofing."[8]

In his first year at the school, Giraudoux took a *Licence-ès-lettres*[9] in general literature, and he then decided to specialize in German literature.[10] An important factor in his decision was the courses that he took with Charles Andler, a professor of German at the Sorbonne. Andler's classes excited the young student, awakening in Giraudoux a sense of infinite possibilities, a feeling for the newness of life. Interestingly enough, Andler was not dealing with the then present-day Germany but rather with the Romantic Germany of the nineteenth century. Giraudoux was eager to discover the country for himself. In his studies, he found himself confronted with a spirit and imagination that went far beyond the orderly, rational training he had received up to that point in France. According to Jacques Body, the young man had fallen into a state of lethargy. He was studying as usual, but was wondering what the value of it all was.[11] The study of German literature renewed his interest. In 1905 he left for Munich, where he planned to write a thesis on August von Platen, a German poet of the nineteenth century. However, the scholarly world was not of the greatest interest to him during his stay in the country. The contact with a different culture and people had a tremendous effect on Giraudoux. He was exposed to a completely new way of life, and he reveled in the possibility of the expansion of his imagination. At the same time, however, as his recently published letters indicate,[12] he was not totally happy. In spite of his new friends and life, he suffered from homesickness and eagerly awaited his return to France.

In June of 1906, he received the *Diplôme d'Etudes Supérieures*[13] toward which he had been working and, after traveling a bit as part of his studies, finally returned to Paris at the end of 1906 to prepare for his *Agrégation*.[14] His interests had changed considerably and he was no longer able to confine himself to his studies. Rather, he enjoyed all of the pleasurable aspects of a young student in Paris; thus, in 1907, Giraudoux failed the difficult examination for the *Agrégation*. Actually, his trip to Munich and various extra excursions had opened up new vistas for him, and he now envisioned a less restricted life outside the university where he could stroll and view the sights, stop at a café for conversation with friends, and develop a more "cosmopolitan" approach to living. Yet, as Albérès notes, Giraudoux never succeeded in forgetting his previous orderly existence, and "he [was] thus destined to live in contradiction between a perfect and limited order and an unreasoned widening of the vision of ... life."[15] He had now begun to experience some of the conflict of the real and the ideal, which was to be the basis of his future writings. Another important event occurred in 1907–1908, when he was sent to Harvard University as an exchange student. Although he was often homesick and cut short his school year at the end, he seems to have enjoyed his stay in the United States. Moreover, the several months he spent there changed him considerably: he became more elegant, more refined, and less timid.

II *The Years of Experience*

Upon his return to France, he accepted a modest position on the daily newspaper *Le Matin,* writing numerous short stories for the paper, most of which were rather ordinary.[16] Nevertheless, the work provided him with the opportunity to meet people in the literary world, some of whom were useful to him in his coming career. In particular, he made the acquaintance of Bernard Grasset, who was unknown at that time but who later published most of Giraudoux's works. Giraudoux now began to write professionally, publishing short stories in various journals and reviews. Many of the stories were then grouped together in 1909 under the title *Provinciales,* his first major work.

Nevertheless, this was a period in Giraudoux's life when he was not ready to settle down to something challenging. In effect, he was still prolonging his youth. His rather carefree, aimless existence reflected in large measure the feelings of the period, at least as we now look back upon *la belle époque.*[17] Superficially, at least, life was a peaceful, joyful experience: no major wars were in progress, a facade of elegant civilization was still extant, literary and artistic endeavors were thriving. Although World War I would soon shatter this tranquility, people were then quite blissfully separated from any harsher reality.

All of this probably helped contribute to Giraudoux's own natural tendency toward noncommitment and evasiveness. As Georges Lemaître notes: "Because reality as he saw it contained nothing truly coherent and solid, how could he become firmly attached to any of its aspects? He therefore displayed a tendency to adopt an elusive, evasive, detached attitude toward life. That 'indifferent' disposition of mind was probably innate in him, but it was certainly reinforced by the nature of the moral atmosphere in which he spent his formative years."[18] This detachment, which he had displayed as a young schoolboy, remained with him into his adult years, and his first writings — like *L'Ecole des indifférents (The School for the Indifferent)* and *Simon le pathétique (Simon, the Sensitive)* — reflected very strongly his evasiveness, a point that many reviewers would criticize. However, as his later works indicated, Giraudoux's "indifference" was simply an early sign of his effort to cope with a reality that he found sordid. All of his writings are an indication of his desire to transcend reality, to go beyond everyday existence to a purer realm.

At this same time, the new writer still had to find some work that would provide him with a steady income, and he was in the process of changing careers. He had not studied hard for the *Agrégation* examination because, consciously or subconsciously, he realized that he did not want to enter the teaching profession. Rather, he decided to become part of the diplomatic corps, and he redirected his efforts to prepare for the examinations in this field. In 1910, he passed the test for the French Foreign Service and was assigned a series of secondary positions that did not demand too much from him.

The next major development in Giraudoux's life was his participation in World War I. The young man served as a sergeant in the 298th Regiment, taking part in the Alsace campaign. The French suffered losses, and Giraudoux's regiment retreated, later participating in the Battle of the Marne, where he was wounded on September 16, 1914. Although his wounds were not major, he was hospitalized, and his injuries were complicated by an intestinal ailment that plagued him for the rest of his life. He returned to active duty for the Dardanelles campaign and, again, was wounded, this time in the shoulder. This second injury, plus his recurring stomach troubles, removed him from active service. While he did not see much action, when he was in battle, he displayed great courage, for which he was later decorated.

Although still in the armed forces, Giraudoux was attached to the diplomatic corps of Philippe Berthelot, who had previously befriended him. Berthelot was now assisting the minister of foreign affairs, Aristide Briand. At this time, in spite of the war, Giraudoux reassumed the sense of dilettantism that was part of his prewar character, and he continued to lead a rather free existence, without too many major responsibilities. He did go to Portugal on a military mission and then was sent to the United States, where he was part of a group of French military instructors at Harvard. Here, he renewed his contacts with his friends and led a fairly easy life. Upon his return to France, he fell ill again with his intestinal problem and had to be placed in the hospital. Until his discharge in 1919, the young officer had relatively undemanding assignments.

However, the war and his experiences in it did affect him to the extent that, as a writer, he produced three works published between 1918 and 1920 dealing with the topic: *Lectures pour une ombre (Campaigns and Intervals), Amica America,* and *Adorable Clio.* If we are to judge from his comments in these works, it does not seem as if the war touched him too deeply, for he displays once again a certain detachment from the actual happening, concentrating instead on the sense of comradeship among the soldiers. Yet, as we know, he always refused to present reality directly, and his seemingly nonchalant attitude toward the war probably reflected his attempt to reduce the horrors of the reality of battle.

Shortly before the war, Giraudoux made the acquaintance of Suzanne Boland,[19] who was to become his wife a few years later. The two met at a party and were immediately attracted to one another. Suzanne Giraudoux noted in an article published in 1950 that she especially liked Giraudoux's intelligence and his feisty, combative spirit.[20] Since this matched her own spirit, she continued, the two people challenged each other often. They were married on February 5, 1921,[21] and they had one son, Jean-Pierre. At this point, Giraudoux was obviously required to change his lifestyle. In his late thirties, with a wife and child to support, he had to think more seriously about his career. In 1919, through a special reclassification from his military service, he was assigned to more important positions in the government, the first of which was his nomination to the rank of secretary of the embassy. But he was immediately forced to ask for a leave of absence because of his poor health, and he returned to recuperate to Cusset, where his parents and his brother, Alexandre, lived. In April 1920, he came back to Paris and was assigned to the Department of French Works Abroad, a branch of government that was established to oversee the growth of French intellectual influence abroad. During the next four years, Giraudoux performed his duties well, eventually becoming head of this unit in 1922.

At the same time, he reached a new level in his writing. Up to this point, his works had been known to a very limited public and did not have much impact. However, during this period, he published *Suzanne et le Pacifique* (*Suzanne and the Pacific,* 1921), *Siegfried et le Limousin* (*My Friend from Limousin,* 1922), and *Juliette au pays des hommes* (*Juliette in the Land of Men,* 1924). These writings revealed an author of substance, and they marked him as a writer of considerable promise.

Troubles in his diplomatic career soon developed. Philippe Berthelot, who had been his long-time protector, came into conflict with Raymond Poincaré, a former president of the republic and currently a senator.[22] Berthelot was involved in a financial scandal that resulted in his disgrace and removal to the inactive list of the ministry. Giraudoux began work on a book to defend his friend against the hostility of Poincaré. The senator then began an attack on Giraudoux and had him sent to Berlin as secretary of the embassy, a post that Giraudoux held only five days, asking to be given a leave for health reasons.[23] Later, after matters had quieted down, he was permitted to return to Paris as head of the Services of Information and Press.

In 1926, Giraudoux finished *Bella,* the book that he wrote to vindicate Berthelot. Poincaré and several of Giraudoux's colleagues were presented in a highly unflattering manner. The result of the publication was to destroy any chances Giraudoux might have had for a successful career as a diplomat. Realizing this, he asked to be placed *hors cadre,* no longer a part of the regular diplomatic staff, and he was appointed to the Commission on the Assessment of Allied Damages in Turkey, an assignment that took relatively little of his time and that he retained until 1934.

Europe was going through a period of relative peacefulness at this time. In 1925, the Treaty of Locarno had been signed, and a spirit of harmony prevailed in relations between France and Germany. In addition, Giraudoux's personal life was happy. Although later years would see a marked breakdown in their relationship, the author and his wife were compatible at this point, and they took great pleasure in their young son. Those who knew Giraudoux at that time also commented upon his amiability and his obligingness. Yet, underneath his surface charm, he still retained many of the same qualities that had been noticed in his younger days: he was still discreet, evasive, somewhat secretive.

III   *The Years of Success*

Giraudoux now began to pursue his writing career more actively, and he turned to the stage, for it offered the opportunity for a larger audience: "I suffered from not being able to express the result of my meditations, of my observations, of my reflections to larger groups."[24] He turned to *My Friend from Limousin,* the novel that he had published in 1922 and a part of which he had previously dramatized for a *festschrift*[25] honoring Charles Andler. This work, which dealt with French-German relationships, was very much a part of the deepest preoccupations of the writer: "The theater offered me an audience. The hour was still serious. All the bridges were broken between France and Germany. . . . I had German friends who felt the peril, they perceived with anguish that the French-German disagreement threatened to bury Intelligence for long years or centuries. It was necessary to express oneself, to make others understand, to be understood."[26]

After meeting the famous actor and director, Louis Jouvet, the two men set to work to turn Giraudoux's novel into a play. Working closely with Giraudoux, Jouvet helped fashion *Siegfried* into first-rate material. Both Giraudoux and his wife had very little hope for success. Yet the presentation of *Siegfried* in 1928 turned out to be one of the major events in French theatrical history. The drama was well received by the critics, who noted that it infused new blood into the theater. They found the verbal inventiveness and the poetic vision a unique adventure, and the public reacted in turn, wholeheartedly supporting the play.

Professionally speaking, the next ten years represented a period of great triumph for the newly discovered dramatist. He became indisputably the major French playwright of the 1930s and his reputation soared. Plays like *Amphitryon 38* (1929), *Intermezzo* (1933), *La Guerre de Troie n'aura pas lieu* (*Tiger at the Gates,* 1935), and *Ondine* (1939) helped to solidify his position, not only in

France but internationally. At the same time, his work in diplomatic circles took a slight turn for the better. After his success with *Siegfried,* he was given a promotion to the rank of councilor of the embassy, and in 1934, he was appointed inspector general of the Diplomatic and Consular Posts Abroad.

However, beneath his apparent good fortune lay a substratum of personal difficulties and anguish, which soon began to appear in his writing. Although he apparently was slow in recognizing the dangers of the Nazi regime, even to the point of expressing a certain admiration for Hitler at the beginning, he nevertheless suffered with the possibility of another French-German conflict. Having devoted so much of his writing to attempts to reconcile the spirit of the two countries, both of which were so much a part of his own inner being, this separation was a special blow to him. The writer was now in his fifties and was passing through some sort of depression about his life and the direction it had taken. For one who had experienced a rather prolonged adolescence, the inevitability of middle age took its emotional toll. Most importantly, his marriage had begun to come apart. According to Jean-Pierre Giraudoux, the couple had numerous arguments. Although Giraudoux was usually somewhat unexcitable, Suzanne Giraudoux was pessimistic and neurotic, according to her son, given to gratuitous sorrow and unreasonableness.[27] At one point, it is possible that Giraudoux thought of divorcing his wife, but, Jean-Pierre states, Giraudoux's elderly mother would never have accepted such an action.[28] However, he did begin spending weeks on end away from the couple's apartment, eventually moving out entirely. Georges Lemaître speaks about this difficult period in the writer's life:

The cumulative effect on Giraudoux's mind of the psychological troubles linked with middle age, of the emotional strain resulting from very serious marital difficulties, and of the intense concern that he felt about the disastrous evolution of French and German politics, brought about in him a severe crisis which completely altered his moral outlook. That phase of Giraudoux's life is often referred to as the "1932 crisis." The crisis actually extended over several years — years that were generally marked by pessimism and sadness.[29]

These forces at work contributed to a noticeably more pessimistic view in his writing. Such plays as *Electra* (1937), *Ondine* (1939), and later, *Sodom and Gomorrah* (1943) portrayed women of strong, sometimes violent will and dealt with the subject of the couple who could no longer find happiness together. At the same time, the writer made a definite turn toward reality and began to consider the problems facing contemporary France, offering possible solutions. These essays were grouped together and published under the title *Pleins Pouvoirs (Full Powers,* 1939). Giraudoux's position as inspector of the Diplomatic and Consular Posts Abroad offered him the type of diversion he needed during this period, and he was able to travel a great deal, which removed him from some of his difficulties. From 1935 through 1938, he undertook a series of trips throughout the world, to Poland, the West Indies, the United States, the Far East, the South Pacific, and the Middle East. With the outbreak of war in 1939, the author was summoned to head the office of French wartime propaganda. As a famous writer as well as a diplomat, he may have had certain qualifications for the post, but basically, he was not suited to the position. He could not deal with the bureaucratic details, and he was too much removed from the people. As Jean-Pierre notes, he was a "pursuer of ideas rather than a man of action."[30] His witty, stylized reactions to the problems of a country facing war were too sophisticated, and he was eventually removed from the position. As the war continued, Jean-Pierre entered the Free French forces, joining General Charles de Gaulle in London. Giraudoux at first worked as curator of historical monuments for the Vichy government, and he desperately wanted to be named commissioner of urbanism, one of his special interests. Although he worked for the Vichy regime for a time, he tried to separate his work from the political aspects of the situation. Later, he withdrew from all activity and, at the family home in Cusset, continued his writing, including *L'Apollon de Bellac (The Apollo of Bellac), La Folle de Chaillot (The Madwoman of Chaillot)* and *Pour Lucrèce (Duel of Angels).*

In 1944, Giraudoux was living in the Hôtel de Castille in Paris, having left his apartment with his wife. Although he did not belong to any Resistance movement during the war, he was now concerned about the dangers of Hitlerism. The full extent of his participation against the Germans is not clear, but there is reason to believe that he was engaged in accumulating documentation on the crimes committed by the German troops in Paris. He was not in good health and suffered from frequent attacks of bronchitis. On November 2, 1943, his ninety year old mother died, and not long thereafter, on January 31, 1944, Giraudoux himself died at the age of sixty-one with severe stomach pains. The cause of his death is not fully

known, and initial rumors, now considered foundless, claimed that
he had been poisoned by the Gestapo. Jean-Pierre, however, has
stated that he believes his father was accidentally poisoned by an
organic product associated with the bad quality of the food of the
period.[31] In addition, since his mother's death, he had been suffering from the flu, and it is possible that his system, always fragile
from a chronic stomach problem, offered little resistance to an
attack of uremia.[32]

CHAPTER 2

The Autobiographical Period

(1909–1920)

L IKE most beginning writers, Giraudoux turned to the experiences in his life as the source of his first literary efforts, and
his writing between 1909 and 1920 is the most overtly autobiographical of any that he would compose. In most of the works, the
central character or narrator can be identified with Giraudoux, and
we learn a great deal about him and his reactions to the world. He
first turned to his existence in the provinces, to Bellac and the
region around it, providing stories of the types of people he knew,
as well as imbuing his tales with the ambience of small town life.
Later, he drew upon his years as a young man in Paris and then at
Harvard University. Finally, his participation in World War I was
an additional source of inspiration.

While most of these beginning efforts cannot compare with his
later, more developed works, the picture that emerges of the young
Giraudoux is totally fascinating and revealing. On the surface, a
feeling of peace envelops the stories. Obviously, Giraudoux the
adult, looking back upon his childhood and adolescent years, had a
nostalgic feeling for that period. His boyhood region of the Limousin would always provide him with a sense of contentment. Bellac
and the surrounding area represented an idyllic period in his life.
The gentle, sloping mountains, the calm rivers and brooks, the
unhurried existence never failed to captivate the heart of the writer,
and this feeling comes through in his early works. When he presents
himself as a young man in Paris, there still remains an enthusiasm
for life. Even in his recounting of the war years, the particular horrors of battle take second place to the pleasures of newly found
friends and comradeship.

Yet throughout all of this, we can begin to detect other aspects of the young Giraudoux. As a child, he is sensitive to the world around him, easily disturbed by its harshness, and at times he seems lonely and isolated. The narrators of the stories begin to appear somewhat detached from reality and, later, as young adults, indifferent. In fact, it soon becomes evident that this indifference is their way of coping with a reality that they do not particularly like. Although they may enjoy life to its maximum, they also prefer to retain an ironic detachment from it and, by so doing, remain superior to it.

Although Giraudoux had not yet clarified in his mind the theme that was to be the basis of most of his writings, the conflict of the real and the ideal, the germ of this point of view can be found in his early writings. Even then, at the time, possibly, of Giraudoux's greatest peace, his characters sense a need for a reality that goes beyond everyday life. Giraudoux the writer found it through his style. Although the subjects of his stories are fairly commonplace, their presentation is unique. Giraudoux's style, which already had strong overtones of the German Romantic writers, is inventive, imaginative, whimsical. It leads in whatever direction its author cares to go, and improvisation, digression, and unexpected analogies form a strong base. Most important, the characters and situations of many of these early works are placed in a cosmic perspective — that is, they are identified through their connection with nature, the seasons, or the elements. In this first period, Giraudoux was doing what he later recommended to his protagonists — he was taking reality and finding the poetry within it. This idyllic part of his life would have all the drabness of reality removed from it by the writer's strongest weapon, his style.

I *The Beginnings*

Although Giraudoux had attempted some earlier essays, his first publication of interest is "Le Dernier Rêve d'Edmond About" ("The Last Dream of Edmond About"), a short story printed in a student review, *Marseille-Etudiant,* on December 16, 1904. This first effort, while not of major significance and somewhat different from his other writings of the period, tells us much about the future author. The story is a dream-fantasy about a soldier in love with a prefect's wife. Their love affair is told through extravagant situations and images in which both countryside and people constantly change amidst passages of mock-lyric and mock-heroic sentences.

In this work, Giraudoux turned to German sources for his inspiration. It was just about this time that Charles Andler's courses at the Sorbonne were revealing the magical, inventive, and ironic world of the German Romantic authors to Giraudoux. It was perhaps understandable that he should turn to the German model, as it suited so perfectly his own natural tendencies in writing. According to Jacques Body,[1] the loose construction, the fanciful humor, and the atmosphere of nightmare and fantasy found in "The Last Dream" are reminiscent especially of the German Romantic novels of E. T. A. Hoffmann.[2] In addition, this early effort by Giraudoux makes us think of the *Märchen,* the German folk tale of the nineteenth century. As Body defines the *Märchen* — "The feeling that nature produces in us during moments of mystery . . . our internal poem . . . the image of the dream in which the impossible, in which precosmic anarchy, is reestablished"[3] — we can understand what attracted Giraudoux to this style of writing. Giraudoux felt a special association with this view of the universe, and the *Märchen,* with its frequent digressions and its unusual juxtaposition of words and images, suited his improvisational style. While Giraudoux's later writings were more controlled and restrained, at this stage in his career, he had abandoned the clarity and the verisimilitude that had been part of his French education for the phantasmagoric and irrational world of the *Märchen.*

He continued to write and published short stories in various journals and reviews. He also worked for the newspaper *Le Matin,* where he and his friend Franz Toussaint were asked to handle the literary page. Both men wrote short stories for the page, as did some of their friends, with Giraudoux publishing several of his under the pseudonyms of E.-M. Manière and Jean Cordelier. From a literary point of view, these newspaper writings of Giraudoux are generally second rate. He was writing for a general public, and he did not follow his natural stylistic pattern. Published in a volume in 1952 with the title *Les Contes d'un matin (Short Stories for a Morning),* the tales, for the most part, do not show any special originality, and many of them are surprisingly realistic and conventional in presentation. However, even in these works of youth, we can see some of the humor and fantasy of the writer, along with a little bit of his verbal extravagance and metaphors.

During this same period, he was involved with the publication of the short stories that made up his first major work, *Provinciales* (1909). Although the stories in this collection were written about the same time as those of *Short Stories for a Morning,* the style is clearly different, suggesting that he was very much aware of the publics for which he wrote and that he aimed his material accordingly. *Provinciales* is made up of short stories of greater substance, and it was accepted by the rising new publishing house owned by Bernard Grasset. Giraudoux's chance meeting with the young philanthropist who founded the publishing firm started his literary career. According to Laurent LeSage, the event occurred one day while Giraudoux was having a drink at a sidewalk café.[4] He struck up a conversation with Grasset, who then told Giraudoux about the authors he had signed for his new publishing venture, asking Giraudoux to submit some of his stories. This fortuitous encounter led to a lifelong commitment by Giraudoux to the firm where most of his major works appeared during his lifetime.

In "The Last Dream of Edmond About," the new author had turned to the German Romantics for inspiration. In *Provinciales,* he drew upon his early boyhood years in the Limousin region. In effect, right at the beginning of his writing career, he utilized the two major sources of so much of his work, Germany and France. The short stories of *Provinciales* are rooted in French life at the turn of the century, and the characters are types Giraudoux must have known during his childhood — the middle-aged spinsters, the civil servants, the young girls. At first glance, the basic outlines of the stories do not suggest anything terribly unusual. "From My Window" recounts the tale of a ten year old boy who watches the activities of a small town from his window while he is recovering from an illness. The people passing by typify life in rural villages, and the boy is particularly intrigued by a man who is scorned by the rest of the town because he is living with a woman to whom he is not married. Another story, "Saint Estelle," tells of a local chambermaid who is dying. However, she supposedly sees the Virgin Mary, fights off the forces of the devil, and is cured. Following this "miracle," the chambermaid is turned into a local saint, and the townspeople force her to enter a convent, much against her wishes. "The Small Duke" relates how a young, friendless boy named Jean finds a companion in another young boy, called *le petit duc.* This boy becomes the idol of Jean's lonely life, until one day Jean, because he is the son of a tax collector, denounces a smuggler. *Le petit duc* disapproves of Jean's action and turns away from him. In "The Pharmacist," a wealthy matron tries to interest a road surveyor in her two eligible daughters. In so doing, she plays a trick on him to take him away from the pharmacist's wife of whom he is enamored.

Each one of these stories could be the subject of a work by Alphonse Daudet, whom Giraudoux had admired at one time. However, instead of merely providing a sentimental, nostalgic look at his childhood, the author places his writing in a broader, more universal context. As René Marill Albérès comments, *Provinciales* establishes what is to be the essential law of the esthetics of Giraudoux: "Place the most minuscule, even the most banal of human life in a cosmic context, see man only in relation to the universe."[5] Giraudoux takes the everyday happenings from his boyhood and gives them a sense of the cosmos; the small moments of the day are placed in a larger setting, linked to the world surrounding them. His characters are closely related to the seasons, to the sun, and references from the animal and natural worlds are frequent.

In almost everything that he wrote, Giraudoux's main preoccupation was the search for something surpassing man's everyday existence. Even the reality of his beloved Limousin area was sometimes marked by a drabness in his mind. He constantly tried to provide a sense of poetry to man's arid existence, to effectuate a cosmic relationship for man and to establish a connection with nature. Moreover, in these first stories, we can also see the beginning of the structural pattern that would predominate in most of his works: the search for the ideal transcending reality, the failure to sustain the moment of the ideal, followed by the somewhat reluctant and stoical return to reality to seek out the poetry to be found therein. In "The Small Duke," Jean's friendship with the new boy becomes a marvelous period in his otherwise lonely existence; but this friendship does not last and he must return to his previous solitary way of life. In "The Pharmacist's Wife," the road surveyor finds the title character so enticing that his life is enriched immeasurably. However, because of the trick played upon him, he loses her, probably forever. Even in "From My Window," the young boy finds his interest awakened by the relationship of the old man and the woman, only to have it end with the man's death.

Provinciales is the first attempt by the author to transcend reality. Later efforts will be more powerfully written, and the writer's basic theme will be clearer. Yet much of the essence of Giraudoux can be found in this early work.

II   *The Young Esthete:* L'Ecole des indifférents

In 1911, Giraudoux published his second work, *L'Ecole des indifférents (The School for the Indifferent),* composed of three short stories that had previously appeared in various journals. The three stories ("Jacques l'égoïste," "Don Manuel le paresseux," and "Bernard, le faible Bernard"), while separate in their plot lines, are unified in that each of the main characters is apparently meant to represent an aspect of Giraudoux as he saw himself at an earlier period in his life. Like many authors when they first begin writing, Giraudoux turned to his own life and drew directly from his own feelings, often describing himself in a rather unflattering light.

During the first decade of the 1900s, Giraudoux tried to grasp all of life's pleasures: he was the esthete, the dandy who paid attention to his clothes, the romancer of the many *jeuenes filles.* If we draw a portrait of the early Giraudoux from what we see in these stories and from what his friends of the time tell us, we know that he was elusive and refused to accept many of life's realities, preferring to remain aloof and indifferent, to enjoy himself without committing too many of his own emotions. It appears that the writer saw these qualities in himself and did not hesitate to describe the main protagonists in these stories — the Giraudoux characters — as selfish, lazy, and weak.

In each of the short stories, there is a slender thread of a story line. "Jacques, the Egotist" deals with a young man in Paris who shows no real affection for anyone, he either mocks other people or is indifferent to them. He is cruel to a good friend who actually shares much of this same indifference toward people; he refuses to allow a girlfriend, Dolly, to become his mistress; he fantasizes about marriage to Miss Spottiswood, the prettiest American in the city. "Don Manuel, the Lazy" takes place at Harvard University, where Giraudoux had recently spent a year studying. Like Jacques, Don Manuel seems to share no deep feelings toward anyone or anything other than his cousin, Renée-Amélie, whom he has not seen since she was a child. When she suddenly appears in Boston to visit him, he discovers to his satisfaction that she does not interest him any more, and he turns his attention to making a conquest of Miss Gregor, an opera singer. "Bernard, Weak Bernard" is a young man of twenty-three in Paris who spends a great deal of his time imagining a better life for himself than that which ordinary reality has provided. For a time, he returns to the small provincial town where he was born, thinking that he may be able to accept the humble joys of this existence. However, he soon returns to Paris to resume his somewhat directionless life.

In all three cases, the central characters are people who have withdrawn from the responsibilities of life — they have removed themselves in one form or another from its realities, having accepted a detachment that has resulted in indifference. Dolly explains this attitude to Jacques: "You are discreet but that is because what happens to others is indifferent to you.... You are like those people who are moved more by the photograph of their friends than they are by their friends themselves."[6] In the cases of Jacques and Don Manuel, the two characters are particularly harsh and cruel toward others. And all three protagonists feel superior to the people around them, implying that the others do not belong in their special lives. Only in Bernard's story do we begin to see some doubts expressed about this aimless existence, this superior detachment that allows no close connection. But even these doubts are somewhat passing, and essentially, the Giraudoux reflected in the pages of these stories is someone who enjoys the irresponsibilities of his existence, someone for whom life is an imaginative fantasy.

In this respect, *The School for the Indifferent* is not very appealing; the characters are unattractive and seem shallow, scarcely worthy of our attention. Yet the stories retain our interest for other reasons. They provide us with a candid accounting of the personality of the writer at an early period in his life and help us to understand his feelings about reality. The superior attitude displayed by his characters at this point is the forerunner of an important trait found in the protagonists of later works. As he continued writing, the author developed the concept of the *élus,* the chosen ones — those people who are superior because they have the ability to see beyond the everyday reality, to perceive the relationship of man and the universe. As a result, the unsympathetic, somewhat arrogant characters of the early works change into the exciting, more profound *élus* of later novels and plays. Finally, Giraudoux's style compensates for many other weaknesses. The author had an unusual ability to take an ordinary situation and, through an unusual comparison or metaphor, to present an original and fresh description. At one point in *The School for the Indifferent,* Don Manuel draws this unusual portrait of Mademoiselle Blanchet, one of the young girls whom he has met: "She is one of the one thousand girls obliged by a mysterious destiny to remain beautiful and resigned in the midst of mediocrities. Never able to attain any of their wishes, they seem more sacred, like statues who no longer have arms. In respect to them, I feel the same remorse or the same regret as I would upon seeing a lamp light up in the windows of a poor chalet'' (*OR* I, 134). Even in his less effective works, Giraudoux's inventive mind and his touch with language turned his writing into an imaginative experience.

III   *The War Literature:* Lectures pour une ombre,
Amica America, Adorable Clio

Although the theme of the dangers of war was to play a significant role in some of Giraudoux's later writings (most notably, *La Guerre de Troie n'aura pas lieu*), the author's early reactions to battle seem curiously muted and even somewhat frivolous, if we are to judge from the three books that came directly out of his participation in World War I: *Lectures pour une ombre (Campaigns and Intervals),*[7] *Amica America,* and *Adorable Clio.* In these accounts, Giraudoux emphasizes not the carnage of the war, but the human, personal side of the soldiers' lives, stressing what took place away from the battlefield.

The first of the three books, *Campaigns and Intervals,* was published in 1917, but a part of it had already appeared in 1916. Most of the material for the work came from diaries that Giraudoux kept while he was a soldier, and the book itself was published while the writer was still on duty. It is divided into three sections: ''The Return from Alsace,'' which recounts the activities of the 298th Infantry Regiment during August 1914, its marches through Alsace, and its return north to take part in the Battle of the Marne; ''Periplus,'' the continuation of the account of this roundabout trip to the Marne via Paris; and ''Five Evenings and Five Awakenings of the Marne,'' which tells of the battle itself in September 1914.

Everything is told from the point of view of the soldier back of the lines. In the march through Alsace, we learn a great deal about the Alsatian villages, people, and countryside. Giraudoux was assigned as an interpreter in the conflict, and most of his duties involved him in activities away from the front lines. Very often, the writer provides picturesque descriptions of the animals, flowers, and vegetables of the region rather than offering any commentary on the conflict. At this point, Giraudoux's company saw relatively little action and was on the periphery of most of the battles. The author cannot always contain his frustration over this: "We are beginning to grow tired of fighting all alone" (*OLD,* 8). He continues: "A bullet, a single bullet passes near us.... A single German pays us the honor of shooting" (*OLD,* 14); "Thus we spend our days between children and old people.... We are conquering a country in which the adult age does not exist" (*OLD,* 23). As a result, references to any harsh realities of the conflict are quite rare. Usually, Giraudoux turns to the poetic image or to a somewhat whimsical view in order to uncover the personal — the humanity of the situation. In spite of his early complaints, Giraudoux did see battle and was wounded on September 14, 1914, but the writer stops his account on September 10 without mentioning his injury. Albérès comments on the importance of this omission: "This precise break in the story just before a wound which Giraudoux never mentioned in his work and which should have constituted the last chapter of an autobiographical war story underlines a desire for modesty which flees realism and confidential information and which, by means of the dignity and the detachment that it indicates, reveals the meaning that he wanted to give to his war diaries."[8]

The second book, *Amica America,* published in 1919, was based upon a military assignment the young man was given to the United States in 1917. Along with other French officers, Giraudoux was sent to Harvard University (where he had once been a student) as an instructor of American officers. The work is composed of a series of short works: "Speech in Massachusetts" is a witty, amusing account of the reception of the young French officers in Boston; "Already We See..." tells of some of the people whom Giraudoux met: Miss Longfellow, Marie-Louise, Muriel Patham; "Rest at Lake Asquam" and "For Groton and Middlesex" recount holidays that he took to the New England countryside; and "Film" deals with the bizarre story of Mae, a sixteen year old girl who wants to die but is kept alive by being introduced to new acquaintances who distract her momentarily from her death wish. America, for the writer, was a place of youth and undoubtedly provided him with a fresh outlook on life. However, Giraudoux's account of his second visit to Harvard is fairly haphazard and offers no precise details of what he did during his stay there. He does enjoy, however, telling about the original and somewhat eccentric people whom he met. Besides the encounter with Mae, mentioned above, he talks of Lee, the poet, who enjoys suffering and is annoyed at the war, for he is no longer the only one in torment; or of Muriel, the dancer, who cannot appear in silent films because she is unable to move her upper lip, and the audience is unable to guess what she is saying. Everything that Giraudoux observes is translated by his imagination into a fanciful, almost absurd report. Banal, ordinary events are transformed into amusing, inventive accounts: at the reception for the young French officers, the president of the society, rising to give a speech, begins with the word "France" and cannot continue because of the ovation that ensues. Each time he tries, he starts again with the name of the country and is again interrupted.

The last of Giraudoux's observations on the war, *Adorable Clio* (1920), is a grouping of diverse essays, taking the reader up to 1919 through the armistice. This particular selection of articles is more disparate than the previous two books and does not follow any time sequence. The two most interesting essays — and most revealing about Giraudoux — are the first and the last: "Night in Châteauroux" and "Adieu to the War." In the first account, perhaps one of the best short works he ever published, the narrator, namely, Giraudoux, is in a hospital in Châteauroux with a suspected attack of appendicitis. He has not been back to the village since his school days, and naturally, he begins to recall his past. While in the hospital, he discovers that a friend of his is also there. In the story, Giraudoux gives this friend the name of Pavel Dolgorouki and says that he is a Russian acquaintance who had been in Munich with him during the narrator's school days. However, Jacques Body maintains that the character is really the prototype for Zelten, later one of the principal figures in *My Friend from Limousin,* but that Giraudoux did not dare give Pavel a German name during the World War I years when he was writing his story.[9]

The author then sets up a fanciful situation in which the two friends spend the whole night in the hospital writing letters back and forth to each other, recalling fondly their past days, although with some anxiety: "Each one eagerly questioned this unexpected mirror which sent one's image back, a mirror-friend, a young image" (*OLD,* 207). In effect, each one is afraid to discover that the other may have grown up, because of the fear that he himself has not done so. In the course of their correspondence, they also begin to establish their own personalities, and the narrator-Giraudoux offers an interesting self-description: "I am surely the poet who resembles a painter the most. I can write only in the mid-

dle of fields; find rhymes only by seeing similar objects; reach the
word which is difficult to grasp only if a man makes a gesture, or if
a tree bends" (*OLD*, 212). In other words, he takes reality as his
original inspiration but will use his inventive, creative imagination
upon it.

Upon his release from the hospital and before his return to Paris,
the narrator has time to wander around the city, and he recalls his
childhood with pleasure. At the same time, he realizes that he has
long since gone beyond that special moment, and he ends his chapter on Châteauroux with these words: "Goodbye, my childhood!"
Actually, the author may have been somewhat self-deluding, because he could never abandon his childhood. And this particular
story is, in its own way, an embryo of his later work, for he is basically dealing with the two major influences on his young life that
would remain with him through his adulthood — France and Germany. Châteauroux represents his early years in France, a period
and country he always cherished. Pavel, the friend from Munich,
symbolizes Giraudoux's student days in Germany. Even at this
stage, the French-German influences, the basis of so much of his
later writing, emerge as central and important themes.

In *Adorable Clio,* as in *Amica America* and *Campaigns and
Intervals,* Giraudoux displays a certain ambivalence toward the
war. On the one hand, he recognizes its horrors, and he himself was
wounded twice. On the other hand, he rarely speaks of these horrors, and most often, he discusses war in a highly whimsical vein.
The reasons for this are clear. It would have been totally alien for
someone of Giraudoux's sensibilities to recount the carnage of
battle directly. He always tried to transcend reality, and this was
obviously the perfect occasion to do so. In actuality, he simply took
a reality that existed — the human story of the men behind the lines
— and through omission rather than invention, talked about the
war. If at times the tone is too lighthearted, it was simply Giraudoux's way of covering up the brutal reality in front of him.

Nevertheless, it also seems clear that there were certain aspects of
the war that he liked. We see an indication of this in the dedication
to *Adorable Clio* when he states: "Pardon me, war, for having
caressed you all the times that I could" (*OLD,* 189). And, the very
last line of the work takes a revengeful tone: "I am a conquerer,
Sunday, at noon," suggesting the excitement and attraction that
war holds for him. In this last section of the book, in the essay
entitled "Adieu to the War," Giraudoux indicates what must have

been the real magnetism of war for him. He describes the end of the conflict by expressing the loss of comradeship and closeness that he felt with his fellow soldiers: "I will no longer sleep on the shoulder of a harness-maker, on the heart of a carpenter.... The head of Chinard, the shoemaker, will no longer fall heavily on my knees, like a shell fallen from a tree, and I will no longer be able to place it near me, gently, by putting my two hands around it" (*OLD* 262). It appears that the fellowship of soldiers who have gone through battle together brought the writer out of his indifference. He was no longer separated from mankind — the war had shown the young man in his early thirties that there was much to be gained from a solidarity with humanity. For once and perhaps the only time in his life, the imperfections of people seemed to have been forgotten. Although his writings on the war do not reveal it directly, the author had made major strides in coming to a deeper appreciation of life.

IV   *The Young Giraudoux:* Simon le pathétique

Simon le pathétique (Simon the Sensitive), Giraudoux's next novel, had an unusual composition. The author began the main part of the work as early as 1911, and a section of it appeared in the newspaper *L'Opinion* in 1914. Everything was interrupted during the war, but the writer picked it up again and continued working, publishing a new version in 1918. Finally, Giraudoux made further revisions, publishing the work again in 1923 and, once more, with further changes, in 1926. In effect, though, the novel is part of the early Giraudoux years and does not reflect the maturing process that the war period brought to the writer. Basically, *Simon the Sensitive* is divided into two parts: Simon's days as a student and his first adventures in the world, followed by the section dealing with his love for Anne. There is little doubt that Simon is very much like his creator. Although the character is fictionalized, the personality is similar to that which we associate with Giraudoux, and Simon's reactions to life help us to understand the young Giraudoux.

In the first part of the work, Simon is a conscientious, industrious student in a small town like Bellac. He has been given a scholarship to a lycée, and he hopes to find his spot in the world, perhaps even to become the president of the republic, as his father suggests. He is to become what his father and his teachers want him to be, to achieve the success that they never had. At the lycée Simon feels, as we suspect Giraudoux must have felt, that he had to be first, to excel in everything.[10] After his lycée days, he is sent to Paris, where he prepares to become a teacher, again doing as his professors wish. However, at this point, Simon rebels and decides that he must travel in order to experience the very things that his professors have been teaching him. They widened his horizons and taught him independence. Now he must put into practice what he has learned. He manages to do well for himself in the world, becoming secretary to Jacques de Bolny, senator and owner of the most influential newspaper in Paris.[11] Later, returning to his small town, he discovers that his old school chum, Gontran, has settled down to the life of an assistant master in a lycée, an existence with little excitement. Simon, on the other hand, has escaped from that humdrum reality. "A little less strength," he says, "a little less indifference, a little less luck and I also would have had this deadly life" (OR I, 649). He has succeeded because he has detached himself from the ordinary reality, approaching the indifference that we saw in Jacques or Don Manuel. Like those two young men, Simon expresses his basic distaste for reality by showing a superiority toward, and a contempt for, his fellow men. This is still the youthful Giraudoux attitude, which has not yet been transformed into the more exciting quest for the unknown seen in the later protagonists, the "chosen ones."

At this point, however, Simon still admits to being attracted to one segment of everyday reality — women. As a young, handsome bachelor, Simon has many female acquaintances: Gabrielle, Hélène, and most importantly, Anne. Anne, who may share some of the traits of Suzanne Boland, Giraudoux's future wife, becomes an ideal creation in Simon's mind. At first, their relationship is full of delights and perfection: "I will speak . . . of the beauty of Anne. It was a beauty too perfect even for her youth. The word beauty is not enough, nor is the word youth, nor the word perfection. She was just as I would have wished her to be had I been fantasy and generosity themselves" (OR I, 668). However, the understanding between the two people soon takes on the normal lovers' difficulties, and arguments and reconciliations ensue. Simon's ideal is further considerably tarnished when Anne announces to him one day that she has previously had an affair. He leaves her for a time, but returns, only to discover that she is now engaged to be married to someone else.

In effect, the first Anne was the perfection that the Giraudoux protagonists seek; she was the paradise away from reality. However, this paradise has been sullied by reality. At this stage in his writing, the author still projects a certain optimism and does not allow imperfection to ruin his hopes. At the end of *Simon the Sensitive,* the young man decides to struggle for his former girlfriend, to reject the disappointment over the purity that has been defiled, and Simon decides that he will still try to marry Anne: "Tomorrow I'm seeing Anne again . . . Will I love her? Tomorrow everything begins again" (*OR* I, 735). At this point, Giraudoux was just beginning to work out the themes that were to be the basis of his future writings. The discovery of the ideal, the inability to hold on to this ideal, the willingness to accept an ideal linked to reality — all of these themes found in his later works were obviously starting to take shape. Along with this, the related question of purity and innocence appears for the first time, later to return in a more pessimistic form in plays like *Judith* and *Pour Lucrèce.*

Although *Simon the Sensitive* is the first complete novel that Giraudoux wrote,[12] one stylistic trait is immediately clear: the writer was not interested in creating three dimensional characters. The protagonists in his works are there to reflect the ideas of the author, and little attention is paid to psychological development. As the various versions of the novel took shape from 1911 through 1926, Giraudoux took whole scenes and speeches from Gabrielle and Hélène and gave them to the constantly expanding role of Anne, who originally was a minor figure.[13] It did not matter to him that the personalities of Gabrielle and Hélène might have been different and that the speeches would not be suitable to the character of Anne. Basically, Giraudoux's protagonists are there to serve his purposes. If we can speak of any character development at all, it is only in the direction of the preconceived "essences" set up by the author and toward which each person must head.

V   *The Schoolboy Parody:* Elpénor

During the last year of the war, Giraudoux wrote *Elpénor,* a parody of Homer's *The Odyssey.* The novel, first published in 1919 and, in another version, again in 1926, recounts in an inventive, gleeful fashion Ulysses' encounters with Cyclops, with the Sirens, and with King Alcinoüs and his daughter Nausicaä. In each case, the tales are told with great verve, and the author takes a schoolboylike pleasure in the exaggerated accounts. For this inspiration, Giraudoux turned to the Hellenic legends that he had studied and obviously appreciated during his childhood. In utilizing these well-known legends, Giraudoux told them in his own way, using anachronisms, contemporary allusions, and constant play on words, very much in the satirical vein of the students of the Ecole Normale Supérieure.

The writer has the greatest fun in inventing a legend for the title character, Elpénor, who actually was an unknown sailor accompanying Ulysses. Giraudoux makes Elpénor, not Ulysses, the protagonist of his tale and uses Homer's citation from the tenth chapter of the Odyssey as his dedication to the work, indicating the parody that he is creating: "Thus died the sailor Elpénor. This is the only occasion that I will have to pronounce his name, for he never distinguished himself, neither by his merit nor by his prudence" (OR I, 187). Since there was no legend surrounding the character, the author was free to create what he wanted. Throughout the novel, Elpénor is provided with imaginary and absurd adventures — he is put to death at the request of Ulysses, then revived by Zeus, and later put to death again by the gods — all told from Giraudoux's bemused, ironical viewpoint.

In one episode, after an accident, Elpénor has been washed up on the shores of the island of King Alcinoüs and his daughter Nausi-caä. When they try to revive him, he happens to awaken at the moment they utter the name "Ulysses." Since they had been told that Ulysses might be shipwrecked and appear on their shores, they immediately assume that this is the famous man. Later, when the real Ulysses arrives, he asks what is taking place. He is told that a festival is taking place to honor "Ulysses" (actually Elpénor). The real Ulysses' reply is typically understated Giraudoux wit: "I understand. My life is composed of such a dense canvas, each episode has been worked out so much ahead of time that they no longer even ask me to live it. Soon, if I don't watch out, it is going to take place without me" (OR I, 245).

Even in this amusing work, Giraudoux inserts the theme of man's desire for the unknown. Ulysses and his sailors are not happy with the island where they find themselves, but are looking for another one, the strange, the unknown having an irresistible attraction. But, as Giraudoux points out, this quest for the unknown can have its drawbacks: "They did not want to see that to possess the second image of happiness was to lust after the third and to deliver oneself to an infinite chain'' (*OR* I, 190). Man may want the unknown, but it may be better to accept the happiness that one has, a view that Giraudoux will expand upon in later works.

It would seem that the author wrote this light-hearted work during a period of relative calm in his own life. At this time, although he was still officially in the military, he was on special assignment and removed from action. He was continuing his relationship with Suzanne Boland, whom he would marry shortly. *Elpénor* was a pleasant, creative diversion for him.

CHAPTER 3

The Typical Giraudoux (1921–1934)

IN 1921, Giraudoux published *Suzanne et le Pacifique,* his best work to date, and from that moment on, he had found the theme that was to be the basis of most of his writing for the next thirteen years. This theme, the conflict of the real and the ideal, had appeared in several of his previous works, from *Provinciales* to *Simon the Sensitive,* but the author had not yet clarified it. Giraudoux's first few writings, although composed when he was an adult, reflected nonetheless his youth, the period before the war, before he had to deal with reality as a mature person. As we have seen, many of these works dealt directly with his childhood, which the author saw in retrospect as a moment of relative harmony. His first contact with Paris, and later with Harvard University, and even his participation in the war were presented as exciting adventures, indicating Giraudoux's sense of discovery. Although he was clearly aware of his need to transcend reality's imperfections, he was nevertheless able to look back upon these years with some satisfaction.

In the second phase of his writing, that period representing Giraudoux at his most typical, the author centers on a time in life when man is passing from the adolescence of his existence, a care-free, somewhat irresponsible stage, to the acceptance of maturity and a deeper awareness of reality. This new phase reflects to some extent Giraudoux's understanding of his own life and its ramifications. He had had an exceptionally long adolescence, if we consider such guidelines as career and family. It was not until 1921, at the age of thirty-nine, that he had married, had had a child, and had assumed more important positions in the diplomatic service that, up to that point, had not occupied much of his time. The writer appears to have had difficulty accepting the responsibilities of maturity, preferring the less demanding existence of his prolonged adolescence.

42

The thrust of his writings during the next several years was in the direction of finding a means of coming to grips with the necessity of reality while still seeking ways to transcend it, leading thus to the conflict of the real and the ideal. He sought an equilibrium in his life, a harmony to the various directions in which his emotions and his esthetics were leading him. While Giraudoux's publications at this stage are often accused of being escapist, they actually represent a very deep expression of his inner feelings, and they are, in their own way, as autobiographical as those writings of the first period — with autobiography now being expressed through the ideas or themes rather than through narration of incidents from his life.

The conflict of the real and the ideal with which he was dealing is basically the situation of man who finds himself restricted within a narrow, limited, drab reality containing no imagination or poetry. The Giraudoux protagonist, usually a heroine, the young girl or *jeune fille,*[1] tries to break out of this confining situation to enter the realm of the ideal, the unknown. She seeks contact with the cosmos, with nature, for she senses that there has to be a more perfect reality, a super reality. Such an attempt on her part is, of course, a type of escape from the real world. But Giraudoux understands that man cannot live only in the world of the ideal, that any such effort will fail. In the final analysis, the ideal is simply a means of learning to deal with reality. Man must accept the real and try to insert poetry and imagination into it, thereby ennobling his existence. This conflict of the real and the ideal is expressed in a wide variety of ways in Giraudoux, probably nowhere so meaningfully to the author as in the novel and stage versions of *Siegfried,* in which, through the symbols of France and Germany, he indicates the two cultures and the two outlooks on life that were so much a part of him. For Giraudoux, France represents his childhood, the rational, logical, classical heritage that he received; while Germany is his young adult life and the intuitive, poetic imagination, the ideal, that he had discovered. It was his feeling that, if he could arrive at a synthesis of these two essential parts of his being, he could also attain the perfection that constantly eluded him.

It is customary to see this period of Giraudoux's writings as a time when he did succeed in finding a compromise and in which a certain harmony has been found between man and the universe, between the everyday life and the cosmos. In addition, in his literary career, Giraudoux was achieving recognition. His novels had garnered a fair amount of attention, although they were still limited to a rather elite public. And his plays were hugely successful, far surpassing his wildest dreams, establishing him as the major dramatist of the period.

Yet underneath, the writer was not totally happy and some of his distress was beginning to show. Even in the most optimistic of writings, like *Suzanne et le Pacifique, Amphitryon 38,* or *Intermezzo,* the endings remain ambiguous, and the compromises seem disappointing. There is always a sense of defeat, and in some of the later works, a decided pessimism overtakes Giraudoux, a pessimism that becomes more pronounced in the final phase of his writing. The hoped for harmony between man and the universe is only superficial, as man becomes more and more aware of the hostile and threatening presence of destiny in his life. The protagonists, often at odds with reality and even with the universe around them, display very definite psychological obsessions. Basic, disturbing problems begin to surface: the question of war and peace, the inability of the husband and wife to form a happy couple, the dilemma of purity and defilement. At this point, these problems generally remained under control, only occasionally flaring up. But the author's sense of harmony and his poetic concept of reality could not last. The presence of a deeper, more tragic view of life was evident, and later works would bring that forth more clearly.

I   *The Basic Theme:* Suzanne et le Pacifique

With *Suzanne et le Pacifique (Suzanne and the Pacific),* published in 1921, Giraudoux found clearly and definitively the theme and structure that he would use in most of his future writings: the flight from humanity, the search for a different reality, the discovery of the ideal; followed by disappointment, and the return to, and acceptance of, humanity. This theme expressed Giraudoux's own deeply felt need for the imaginative world, away from reality, and represented his attempt to find a balance between his desired ideal and the reality in which he had to live. In this work, for the first time the writer utilizes the young girl, the *jeune fille,* as his main character, probably because he saw her adolescent state as an appropriate period in life for revery. It is also probable that Giraudoux felt that he should no longer present his ideas through a semi-autobiographical hero, as he had done in *Simon the Sensitive,* for his writing now touched upon his emotions as an adult, not safely removed in the world of childhood as his earlier works had been. The discreet and reserved novelist undoubtedly did not want to disclose too much of himself.

Suzanne is an eighteen year old girl from Bellac, shortly before World War I, who has just won first prize from the *Sydney Daily* newspaper in Australia for the best maxim on boredom, with her entry: "If a man is bored, . . . give him excitement; if a woman is bored, hold her back" (*OR* I, 260). Her prize is a trip around the world, and she takes off with much eagerness, for she has always been fascinated by foreign countries. Heading first to Paris, she becomes acquainted with the city and meets Simon and Anne (the same two characters from *Simon the Sensitive*). Then she sets sail, making new friends on board ship. A violent storm occurs in mid-Pacific and only Suzanne survives the wreck, finally reaching the shore of an isolated island. While she experiences preliminary difficulties on the island, she soon learns to adjust her way of living to the pace of her new-found land, and in Giraudoux's whimsical version, she leads a relaxed, contented existence. In a parody of God's creation of the world, Suzanne spends her first six days doing nothing but preparing her bed. After a year, surrounded by luxuriant nature and exotic animals, she decides to swim to a nearby island. Upon reaching it, she finds indications that someone was there before her and that, like Robinson Crusoe, this person had been very active, doing his best to make his life like the existence he had known before being shipwrecked, reshaping nature to suit his needs. Later, Suzanne compares her imaginative life, perfectly in tune with nature, to the frenzied type of existence led by Robinson Crusoe ("the only man, perhaps, . . . that I would not have liked to meet on an island").[2]

Returning to her own island, Suzanne suddenly feels a need for some contact with humanity. She dreams of a man, "a tall, young, blond man with big, dark eyes," and she longs for him to hold her. She begins to forget how to spell and no longer remembers names easily. In order to recapture her past life, she assigns names from her small village of Bellac to the tropical nature surrounding her, soon developing her own little universe. She composes letters to Simon and invents his replies as well, so that she can keep up the facade of contact with human reality. Eventually, the outside world returns to Suzanne. It comes back slowly: she finds dead bodies on

the island, victims of World War I; she reads a newspaper that she
has found, that tells her what is going on in the war; finally, she is
discovered by some astronomers who have come to the island to
view an eclipse. Upon her return to France, she responds willingly
to the lure of humanity, and French ambience calls her back to the
real world, especially when she meets the controller of weights and
measures, a character whom Giraudoux used again in *Intermezzo*.

Suzanne and the Pacific is a typically fanciful Giraudoux tale,
accompanied by digressions and stylistic devices. Whimsical, amus-
ingly inventive, it is more deeply felt than it may seem at first. Although the writer regarded reality with detachment, he was pro-
foundly aware of its imperfections and felt a strong need to escape.
Suzanne is, of course, the symbol of this need. By the device of the
shipwreck, Giraudoux places her as a stranger in a new environment, a situation frequently repeated in his works. Having been
thrust out of the normal pattern of her existence, she creates a new
life for herself within the open framework of nature. But it soon
becomes apparent to Suzanne — and to Giraudoux — that such an
attempt is not satisfactory. She is alone, isolated, lost. She begins to
feel deceived and almost smothered by nature. At times, especially
during her visit to the second island, nature becomes an enemy,
actively hostile, trying to humiliate her. In effect, though, nature is
simply preparing her for what is to take place — her return to the
real world. Even though Giraudoux sees links between the two
realms, he is also aware of a radical separation between the two and
understands that man cannot live only in the ideal. As Charles P.
Marie points out, "the world about which Giraudoux speaks in his
writings, although it seems to flee reality by its search for dream
and abstractions, actually probes it [reality] and ponders it and . . .
he gives it the depth that understanding alone can provide."[3] The
resolution of the problem is found in Suzanne's return to France
and her rediscovery of the values of reality. Having had her fling
with the unknown, she now seems willing enough to accept a compromise. Nature and the animal worlds are waiting in France to
help lead her back to her normal life. A little afraid, a trifle disappointed, Suzanne will forget everything when she meets the controller of weights and measures, for he will help her uncover the
poetry and imagination in reality.

Laurent LeSage suggests that the tale represents a passage of the
protagonist from adolescence to maturity,[4] and this is very likely
the case. For the moment, Giraudoux accepts reality as part of the

process of maturity. But this compromise is tenuous and filled with some deception. Later, the fragile agreement will come apart.

II   *The French-German Entente:* Siegfried et le Limousin

Having once established the theme that would be the basis of his writings, Giraudoux now turned to the two sources that most represented this theme in his own inner being: France and Germany. France was the country that he loved, the country of his family, the country in which he had his roots. It had given him the rational, logical training in which he had managed to find a certain sense of harmony and equilibrium as a child. Then, his first contacts with German studies and his first visit to Germany in 1905 had helped develop new aspects of his personality, presenting the young man with a dynamic, unrestrained, intuitive approach to life and allowing for a poetic interpretation of the universe, an imaginative communion with nature. France and Germany symbolized very deep-rooted sides of Giraudoux's personality, and it was natural that he should use the two countries as bases for his writing. *Siegfried et le Limousin (My Friend from Limousin),* [5] published in 1922, represents the most ambitious work undertaken by the novelist up to that point. The search for a French-German entente indicates Giraudoux's need to find an equilibrium in his soul, an accommodation within his own being.

The author also used the occasion as a moment to meditate on a friend of his who had died during World War I. Giraudoux has stated that the title character, Siegfried von Kleist, was based on André du Fresnois, a writer and critic who was very active in the literary circles of that time, having founded one journal and written for several others. [6] Giraudoux and he were good friends — in fact, they were almost like twins, having the same stature and bearing, and possessing similar personal traits. [7] Du Fresnois disappeared in action in 1914 and was presumed dead. Giraudoux was much affected by this incident, and his first writings on the war, *Campaigns and Intervals,* were dedicated to "André du Fresnois, missing in action." Moreover, Giraudoux indicated that he developed the story line for *My Friend from Limousin* from du Fresnois's disappearance. In the novel, a French soldier, Jacques Forestier, has been wounded and is picked up by the Germans. Suffering from amnesia, he cannot remember his identity. Because his uniform has been ripped away, the Germans have no way of identifying him, but they assume that he must be a fellow countryman. They retrain him, and he is given a new name, Siegfried von Kleist.[8] During the war, it was not unusual for soldiers to suffer from amnesia, and Giraudoux's own brother had experienced it.[9] However, Jacques Forestier's characterization basically comes from du Fresnois (with a little bit of Giraudoux himself thrown in), and through literary means, Giraudoux returned his friend to life as Siegfried.

One other source played an important role in the development of the story. While Giraudoux was writing *My Friend from Limousin,* he was working in the branch of the diplomatic services that dealt with French influence abroad. As a result, he was very much aware of a problem that was preoccupying diplomats at that time. In this period following World War I, responsible people on all levels of government were becoming increasingly concerned over the need for a resolution of the French-German conflict, which was beginning to build up once again. In view of the terrible destruction that both nations had suffered during the previous war, it was essential to avoid future hostilities, to harmonize the two quite different mentalities. Giraudoux's work recognizes this difficulty and makes an effort to explore these two peoples to see if a means of agreement exists. The novel is, therefore, the first time that the author recognizes some of the realities of the political world, the first time that his professional life as a diplomat merges with his professional life as a writer.

My Friend from Limousin begins in France when the narrator, Jean, reads some of the writings of Siegfried von Kleist and recognizes a striking similarity with the articles of his former friend, Jacques Forestier, whom he had presumed dead. Jean contacts Zelten, an exuberant German living in Paris who is constantly working toward French-German unity. Zelten helps Jean leave for Germany to investigate the matter. Claiming to be a French-Canadian called Chapdelaine, Jean becomes Siegfried's French tutor, and he immediately recognizes von Kleist as his friend Jacques. Siegfried has now become an important figure in postwar Germany, having helped the country through many crises. In effect, he has achieved a union of the two cultures — he has been reeducated with the intuition and perceptions of Germany, but has also retained the logic and clarity of his earlier training in France. As a result, he has been able to provide some semblance of order to the rather disorderly process of German politics.

The novel then develops a number of rather complicated subplots, notably the contrast between Geneviève Prat, a French sculptress and the former wife of Zelten, and Eva von Schwanhofer, Siegfried's nurse and the symbol of modern Germany in the novel. Both women have considerable influence over Siegfried, as a struggle develops over whether he will remain German or return to France. A decisive moment occurs when the strong-minded Zelten tries to take over the government of Germany in a *pütsch*. Because he is ultimately defeated, partly through Siegfried's opposition, Zelten reveals the lie that Siegfried has been unintentionally living all of these years and discloses that Siegfried is really French. Siegfried, or now Forestier, returns to France, where his memory is restored by the everyday sights and sounds of his native Limousin region. Upon discovering his true identity, Forestier is torn, like Giraudoux himself, between the virtues of the two countries. Having known the values of the clarity and lucidity of the French mind, he has also experienced the sensations of the intuitive, impulsive German *esprit* and found it to his liking.

Yet, in the final analysis, there is never any real doubt as to which side will win in the conflict. As presented by Giraudoux, France is clearly the more attractive of the two countries.[10] The Germany that the narrator, Jean (as well as Giraudoux), esteems is actually an ideal that does not exist, and Giraudoux regrets the fact.[11] The narrator offers this reaction to the country: "Germany is a great, human and poetic country, which most Germans can easily do without today but to which I have not yet found anything equal" (*OR* I, 401). The Germany that the narrator admires is that of the past. Instead, the real Germany is one in which industry plays a major role and from which poetic feeling has disappeared, a "modern" Germany that is not interested in creating a union with France and in which the people are perfectly willing to call Balzac "a brute, Racine a swine and Molière an oaf" (*OR* I, 458). Moreover, the characterization of the Frenchman, Jacques Forestier, is sharply defined right from the beginning, and he has substance and reality. Siegfried, the German side of the personage, never really exists. He is a symbol, but he has no decided presence in the novel. As a character, he is fairly passive in relation to the action, and in fact, the narrator Jean, obviously Giraudoux himself, plays a much greater role in the work.

There is one character, however, who offers a possible fusion of the French and German qualities. Zelten, a German living in Paris, is first presented as a romantic, mysterious, poetic figure of Old

Germany. He incarnates the Germany of the imagination: "He had blond, curly hair, he sacrificed each minute of his life to dreams, he went into the basins of water fully clothed in order to put his hand in the stream of water or to place the beak of the sleeping swan under its good wing; he was Germany" (*OR* I, 402). At the same time, he loves France and hopes to establish a government in Germany in which the first law will involve a French-German agreement. When he does try to set up such a government, he fails, and this failure also results in Siegfried's downfall. Zelten may represent Giraudoux's hopes that a union of the two sides can be achieved, but his defeat, along with Siegfried's return to France, indicates a pessimistic attitude on the part of the author in this matter.

My Friend from Limousin contains so much of Giraudoux that it enthusiastically brims over with ideas, information, and opinions. The novel is extremely important in the author's works precisely because it is so deeply felt on his part. The subject of France and Germany remained in his mind for several years, and he reworked the theme several times in shorter writings before he eventually chose it as the basis for his first play in 1928. Given this background, it is surprising to learn that Giraudoux wrote *My Friend from Limousin* in a relatively short period of time in 1922, perhaps taking as little as three weeks during a vacation.[12] It is also somewhat surprising that he undertook the composition of the work at the urging of his editor, Grasset. A new award, the Balzac Prize, was going to be given in the fall of 1922, and Grasset wanted Giraudoux to submit an entry.[13] The writer had a reputation throughout his lifetime of being able to write with prodigious ease, and the rapidity with which he prepared this long novel is truly astonishing. At this point in his career, he apparently spent little time rewriting, but composed a great number of chapters or sections of the book, using what he felt he needed and discarding the rest or using it at a later time in another work. His efforts paid off, for he won the prize, although he shared it with another author.

Nevertheless, it would be a mistake to underestimate the significance of the novel. Undoubtedly, one of the reasons that he was able to finish it so rapidly was that the theme was such a profound part of his inner being. France and Germany symbolized his lifeblood, and it was easy for him to develop the substance of the novel. In the following decade, when it became clear that the two countries were not going to be able to resolve their differences and that war was about to break out, Giraudoux suffered considerably. It would mark the end of a dream — a dream that he had first expressed in 1922 with *My Friend from Limousin.*

III   *The Young Girl and Her Escape:* Juliette au pays des hommes

Giraudoux's next work, *Juliette au pays des hommes (Juliette in the Land of Men),* published in 1924, is related in theme to the earlier novel, *Suzanne and the Pacific.* Once again, the central character is a young girl seeking adventure in the world, eventually realizing that she must accept a limited but still poetic reality in her everyday life. Once more, the young girl represents the adolescent stage where life has infinite possibilities, but she finds that the ideal of her dream world is not to be found, and her flight from reality comes to an end.

In the small provincial town of Aigueperse, Juliette is planning to marry Gérard, a young man quite satisfied with, and even proud of, his humble, ordinary life. Juliette, on the other hand, is unhappy, and her curiosity obliges her to search for what the world may offer. Finding Gérard too limited, she decides to leave him for a month before their marriage so that she may have a final fling in Paris. As Giraudoux whimsically observes: "In short, this was the story of an old, young man of twenty, next to a young girl of twenty thousand years; this was the story of life in the province" (*OR* I, 544).

Through the years, Juliette has kept a diary of all the men who have crossed her path and whom she might have married. She now decides to find them to see what has become of them. In the course of her search, Juliette encounters a varied assortment of people, offering Giraudoux the opportunity to satirize modern life. She meets a botanist who has lost contact with the world because he is only aware of rare and unknown plants, a man in Chantilly who lives only by the pride that rules his existence, an archeologist who is lost in his own obscure domain of little interest, a writer who tries to introduce Juliette to his bizarre theory of the *monologue intérieur,* and an amorous Russian who attempts to seduce her.

She discovers that each of these types is a grotesque exaggeration of life. Each one has forsaken the real values of living by devoting himself to only one small part of life. The botanist knows only his few plants, the writer has his *monologue intérieur,* which Juliette realizes is "only slightly different from the sentences of old men who speak to themselves all alone" (*OR* I, 590). In addition, she sees that her visit to the writer has ended in "the defeat of psychology, of psychophysiology, and in the death of style" (*OR* I, 592). Even in the case of Boris, the passionate Russian lover, he is so inept at conveying his different moods that, in Giraudoux's very fanciful version, at a certain moment he decides that he will love Juliette only like a brother and not with passion. He leans over to give her a friendly embrace, and Juliette, misunderstanding his intentions, stabs him!

The young woman is now glad to return to Gérard, who does not have any past or any mysteries, whom she has known since her childhood, and who represents all the values with which she is familiar. Having seen the great world, she has discovered that the true function of man is to accept his limited role in life. Man's imagination may allow him to surpass his normal situation, but this cannot last — he must find the unknown within reality. Surprisingly enough, Juliette finds that Gérard has managed to do this. Upon her return to Aigueperse, she comes upon him bathing naked in a brook, peacefully at one with nature. She suddenly becomes aware that this contact with nature is an indication to her of the ideal within the real. He may be provincial, but he is alive, and the botanist and archeologist in Paris seem old and withered. However, once again, Giraudoux displays his fondness for irony, contradiction, and ambiguity. At the final moment, when Gérard comes to Juliette to embrace her and welcome her back, she plunges into the brook "filled with affection, friendship, and love," implying that there may still be a part of her that is not able to accept Gérard's world totally.

Since *Juliette in the Land of Men* is so similar to *Suzanne and the Pacific,* it does not offer anything new to Giraudoux's work. As with all his novels, however, it does allow him to display his delightful style with its many digressions and its unexpected associations on a series of bizarre and unusual characters. In addition, the author does include one highly interesting section that is quite extraneous to the action but that provides a fascinating glimpse into his conception of his art. In Chapter Six, Juliette is talking to the narrator (presumably Giraudoux), and he lets her read an essay he has been working on called "Prayer on the Eiffel Tower."[14]

In the essay, the narrator is on top of the Eiffel Tower, thinking about the different perspective that life assumes from this height. He is reminded of a former visit to the tower as a student with one of his lycée teachers, Jules Descoutures-Mazet. In thinking of Descoutures, the narrator remembers that the teacher tried to instill certain artistic principles into him. Descoutures detested the Romantics with their exaggerations and their adjectives. Although the narrator-Giraudoux confesses his love for adjectives, he nevertheless avoided them at that time in order to follow his teacher's precepts. In fact, he and his classmates all tried to avoid adjectives, and the only way they could replace them was by using metaphors, a habit that the young Giraudoux carried over to his adult writing. The narrator confesses that he was not able to follow everything that his teacher told him — he did not accept reason with the same passion, nor could he choose between stoicism and epicurianism as Descoutures had wished, since both philosophies held a certain appeal for him. In analyzing what he has done with his writing, the narrator sees himself as the messiah for small objects and animals, for the spots of sunlight — namely, he is the messiah for the world of the imagination. He does not see that he has contributed anything to the progress of the universe from a practical point of view, but he has provided a "certain new way of approaching children and small animals and of speaking about them in their presence. A certain way of offering, instead of one's mouth to another mouth, one's language to another language" (*OR* I, 602). In other words, he has provided humanity with a sense of style, and, he continues, he has furnished everything that is ephemeral and poetic.

In these very few pages placed in the middle of *Juliette,* Giraudoux has offered us an accurate and incisive portrait of himself as an artist, he has given us his *art poétique.*

IV   *The Novel of Vindication:* Bella

Giraudoux had now begun to achieve some recognition as a writer, particularly after the publication of *My Friend from Limousin.* However, at the moment, writing was not his main career — he was part of the diplomatic service and had held a number of posts. From 1920 to 1924, he belonged to the Department of French Works Abroad, a section dealing with French intellectual influence overseas, very much like today's cultural relations division, and in 1922, he was made head of this important department. In actuality, though, Giraudoux was not a terribly hard-working member of the diplomatic corps.[15] He was often absent, or arrived late, or did not arrive at all. He spent a good deal of his time writing his novels while at work, and he would often read what he had written to his aides, asking their opinions and interrupting what they were doing. His presumed profession interested him much less than his literary vocation. About this time, consciously or not, he made a decision that ruined any possibility of a distinguished career in the diplomatic service.

Throughout his years in government, Giraudoux had been protected by Philippe Berthelot, a career diplomat of some importance. Berthelot and Giraudoux had much in common, and the older man watched over the younger one, doing what he could to help along Giraudoux's career. Near the end of 1921, however, Berthelot came under attack from Raymond Poincaré, a former president of the republic, who was at that time a senator and a strong supporter of the conservative position that France must be forceful in its dealings with Germany. Berthelot had been a backer of Aristide Briand, a leading advocate of international peace. Briand had led the French government briefly, but fell from power in 1922 when Poincaré took over as prime minister. Poincaré immediately took advantage of the occasion to dismiss Berthelot. In his official duties, Berthelot had gone to the aid of a major French bank in China that was in danger of collapsing because of an internal dispute. As it happened, one of the bank's directors was Berthelot's brother, and naturally, a charge was made that he had used his influence because of family connections. Berthelot was found guilty and placed on the inactive list of the ministry. Later on, in 1924, after Poincaré's government fell, Berthelot was reinstated and cleared of the charges. After Giraudoux had heard what had happened, he was outraged and decided to write a novel to avenge his friend and protector. In the meantime, Poincaré, aware of Giraudoux's antagonism, had him sent on assignment to Berlin.[16] Although he loved Germany, for the writer this was tantamount to exile — he never wanted to be assigned anywhere but to Paris and he sought revenge through his literature.

Bella, the result of his anger, is the story of a dispute between two important political families: the Dubardeaus (Berthelot) and the Rebendarts (Poincaré). The novel is recounted in the first person by Philippe Dubardeau (the Giraudoux character), son of René, one of the members of the Dubardeau family. The account relates the differences between two types of people, both from the French upper classes. The Dubardeaus are sensitive, cultured, free spirits, and like many of Giraudoux's main characters, they have found a certain peace in their existence by following the natural rhythms of life. The family is composed of six brothers who represent a wide range of interests: René is a diplomat, a second brother is a physicist, another a director of a museum of natural sciences, a fourth a surgeon, still another a minister of finances, and a final one an astronomer. Since they have such varied interests, when they discuss important issues, Philippe observes that it is like "humanity talking to itself." The family lives in Paris, but it has no particular ties to any one region, as Philippe notes: "The six brothers had acquired the talent of making themselves at home in the middle of any country.... My uncles and my father were simply inhabitants of France" (*OR* II, 11). Finally, they are a joyous family, living life to its full measure, seemingly in harmony with the world around them.

In sharp contrast, the Rebendart group has a narrow vision. It lacks the wide contact or appreciation of the world seen in the Dubardeaus. The men are all lawyers, and within their profession, they deal with criminal cases, which results in their deep distrust of humanity. At the same time, they have unlimited respect for the law and see themselves as totally honest. They are "all upright, all intransigent, with their health and their work, always dressed in black, never displaying any of their numerous decorations, but arrogantly wearing over their clothes, visible a hundred meters away, those internal decorations which are named duty and integrity" (*OR* II, 31). They operate only by rules and logic and, lacking imagination, cannot comprehend how the universe might function. Although they are strongly attached to French provincial life, there is no family warmth. And, in their march toward "honor," they are not above deception. If any member of the Rebendart family lacks the qualities that they esteem, he is placed out of sight. Philippe Dubardeau comments cynically: "Accustomed as they were to scorning one of their own, they also scorned all of humanity" (*OR* II, 32).

Naturally, two such different groups have nothing in common, and the Rebendarts are particularly hostile to the Dubardeaus. In the midst of these two conflicting families, Giraudoux sets up a romantic entanglement. Bella, the widow of the son of the minister of justice in the Rebendart family, falls in love with Philippe Dubardeau, a love that must be concealed because of the families' feud. The conflict reaches its peak when one of the members of the

Rebendart clan has come into possession of some documents that will presumably prove that René Dubardeau was involved in a bribe offer. Although René's action was quite proper, it could look to outsiders as if the Dubardeau family were involved in an illegal situation. Through this means, Bella's father-in-law hopes to obtain vengeance on this family whom he so detests. When he is ready to present his proof officially, the documents are missing. Bella announces that she has destroyed them because of her love for Philippe. She then attempts to reconcile the two families. Dubardeau is willing to forget the past, but Rebendart refuses, and following this, Bella collapses and dies.

Interestingly enough, the novel does not end with the death of Bella. At this particular point, Giraudoux adds another chapter, picking up the character of the Baron de Fontranges, Bella's father, introduced earlier in the novel. The author recounts Fontranges' sadness at the death of his daughter in a lyrical and tender manner. Ending the work with Fontranges may have developed from Giraudoux's interest in the theme of the generations and their relationship in view of his own situation as a parent. However, it is more likely that the author became involved with the character of Fontranges and assigned a greater importance to him than originally planned. Moreover, he continued to use Fontranges as a major figure in later works such as *Eglantine* and *Aventures de Jérôme Bardini*.

René Marill Albérès has noted that *Bella* seems to break the cycle in Giraudoux's novels in which the theme usually is a conflict between the cosmos and the real.[17] While it is true that the novel was written for a very specific purpose growing out of Giraudoux's life, the vindication of Berthelot, *Bella* nevertheless fits into the normal pattern of Giraudoux's writings, and we can see how the work still reflects the conflict of the real and the ideal. The Rebendarts symbolize the side of the novelist attached to his past, to the values of provincial life, to order and logic. The author purposely distorts and exaggerates this side in his presentation, making the family seem reactionary and narrow-minded, because he wants to make his point about Poincaré. Nevertheless, the basic attachment to clarity and reason expressed by the Rebendarts was definitely an important part of Giraudoux and his life. The Dubardeaus, on the other hand, typify the pleasures of life and the freedom of spirit that the author sought for Juliette and for Suzanne. And, once more, a girl, Bella,[18] attempts to bring the two sides together. This time, though, all efforts at unity fail, and Bella's death is the overt sign of this failure. Indeed, the choice of death as an end to the situation is somewhat unusual in Giraudoux's writing, suggesting a stronger disappointment than usual with reality. Such an ending also prefigures the somber and pessimistic tones of the later works.

The publication of *Bella* in 1926 created a scandal within diplomatic circles, and with it, the novelist lost any hope of major success in his career, although this may not have been of great concern to him. Besides presenting the dispute between Berthelot and Poincaré, the author also incorporated a number of lightly disguised portraits of people who worked in the government bureaucracy at the time, these portraits oftentimes becoming what some people considered cruel caricatures. Many of Giraudoux's colleagues resented someone taking his personal grievances to the public in such a manner. In addition, at the time of publication, Poincaré had temporarily fallen from power in the turbulent, topsy-turvy world of French politics, and Berthelot had already returned to duty. As a result, it did not look as if Giraudoux had been engaged in doing anything courageous. Berthelot himself may have felt more embarrassed than gratified, for he probably did not especially care to have his dealings in the bank affair brought to public attention one more time.[19]

V *The Fontranges Story:* Eglantine

While he was writing *Bella,* Giraudoux was also working on the novel *Eglantine* (1927), which continues the story of the Baron de Fontranges. Having become fascinated with Fontranges and with the milieu of the nobility, the author was reluctant to drop the two topics, and he began composing this second work. It is quite possible that he may have even planned to incorporate parts of this Fontranges story as sections or chapters into *Bella.* However, *Eglantine* soon assumed its own quite different direction from that of the earlier novel.

In this new work, Fontranges and Emmanuel Moïse, a banker and faithful friend of the Dubardeau family (Moïse is also a character in *Bella*), have both fallen in love with Eglantine, the foster sister of Bella. The story revolves around the love of the two older men (both in their sixties or near) for the young girl, and for the first time, Giraudoux begins to explore in some detail the ramifications of love, a topic that he continued in later works. This time, the writer centers on the bizarre effects that love can have on human beings and on the strange actions that follow. The novelist delves into Eglantine's hold over both Fontranges and Moïse and the resultant obsessions and jealousies. In Giraudoux's version, love assumes many unusual forms and shapes. Fontranges visits Eglantine's room during the early morning hours when she is sleeping because "he never wanted to see her during the day; he wanted to have the illusion that she never woke up, that he was observing the life of a young girl who did not open her eyes" (*OR* II, 131). Moïse is shown as equally capable of singular actions. He goes to Turkey to open and inaugurate a new telephone line between Istanbul and Paris, and the first number he tries to call is that of Eglantine, who is not at home. Because of his fear that she is with Fontranges, he refuses to make any of the necessary protocol calls, tying up the new line for an hour, while he tries unsuccessfully to contact Eglantine. In the cases of both men, Eglantine's departure for one or the other leaves them in such a state that, for a time, they withdraw from the world and remain indifferent to life.

The object of their interest, Eglantine, retains most of the qualities of the *jeunes filles* of Giraudoux. While she is supposedly the mistress of both men, she remains quite virginal or, more to the point, asexual. Giraudoux never presents the love of Eglantine and the older men in any sexual manner, and her relationship with them is generally described without physical contact. She is attracted to elderly men for a different reason: "A terror of change, a strong desire for permanence made her love them for that which was unchanging and definitive: old age. That was the only promise that nature or God kept: men grew older" (*OR* II, 192–93). She is at that point in her young life when she still has to find an identity — and the prospect terrifies her. Fontranges and Moïse represent an ideal for her, they have the stability that comes with age — they will not change. Like Suzanne and Juliette, who sought their ideal, Eglantine finds hers with these older gentlemen and in the reassurances of old age. But, her commitment is really nothing more than a withdrawal from the realities of life, an attempt to escape the vicissitudes of the years of living that she has before her. Like all of the young girls in Giraudoux's work, she has to pass through this phase in her life before settling down to the real world. This point is emphasized at the end of the novel, when Eglantine realizes that she must leave this "pure" realm of Fontranges and Moïse. She now recognizes the inevitability of change, she will return to enter the "terrible convent of humans," a future that she accepts but with considerable reluctance.

Giraudoux's presentation of love is subtle, oftentimes penetrating and always unique. In style and content, it bears some resemblance to Marcel Proust's prose on this same subject. But, in the final analysis, it does not interest the reader to any great extent. The characters and their love are too bizarre, their relationship is presented too coldly and too abstractly. We do not have any sense of life in this world created by the novelist, and even though it does transcend reality, it is not superior to ordinary existence. Fontranges and Moïse suffer from their love, and this sense of suffering must have been shared by the author. Yet, it is not really communicated to the reader.

At the same time, Fontranges and Moïse have another important role in the novel: they are meant to symbolize two different world cultures. Fontranges is supposed to be an example of Western civilization, while Moïse, who was born in the Middle East, is to represent Eastern culture.[20] When Eglantine moves from one man to another, she is also moving from one civilization to another, a structural approach that Giraudoux had used in the Siegfried stories. In *Eglantine,* the approach is less effective. The East-West differences are not distinctly made, and eventually, they do not seem to be a very important part of the book, fading into the background. In *My Friend from Limousin,* the conflict of two countries or cultures came out of a deep-rooted feeling on the author's part. In this novel, he does not seem to be sufficiently interested.

VI *The Novelist Becomes a Dramatist:* Siegfried

It is not hard to imagine the reaction of theatergoers in 1928 when they heard that Jean Giraudoux was writing a play. Up to this time, Giraudoux had been a novelist of some prominence, but his reputation was basically limited to the literary elite. The whimsical inventiveness and the poetic digressions of his works hardly indicated that he would be able to be successful in the theater. Moreover, his somewhat complicated style seemed to be irreconcilable with the more limiting demands of the stage. But, those who foresaw difficulties for the novelist in the theater were wrong — Giraudoux made the transition with extraordinary ease. Undoubtedly, much of the credit for the rather startling transformation belongs to Louis Jouvet, the actor-manager-director whom Giraudoux had met in 1926 and with whom he shared a lifelong collaboration. Jouvet had been a disciple of Jacques Copeau and of his Théâtre du Vieux-Colombier, an important theatrical influence in the first part of the twentieth century. Jouvet had left the Vieux-Colombier in 1924 and was manager of the Comédie des Champs-Elysées theater when he met Giraudoux. Constantly seeking new authors to present, Jouvet asked Giraudoux if he would be able to provide him with some work, perhaps a short play based on *My Friend from Limousin.*

It was natural that Giraudoux should have followed up on this suggestion. In 1924, he had already dramatized a scene from the novel for publication in a collection of articles honoring Charles Andler, his former German professor. In addition, a number of his acquaintances had been encouraging him to continue with the dramatization.[21] More significantly, though, the novelist thought of *My Friend from Limousin* because it remained such an important part of his own life. As we stated before, the question of the French-German relationship was a reflection of Giraudoux's deepest personal preoccupations, and he greatly hoped to find a way to merge the qualities found in the two cultures. Moreover, the political situation of the two countries provided a fine topic for dramatic conflict as the subject of French-German similarities and differences was very much on people's minds in 1927.[22] The theater was, in Giraudoux's mind, the best forum in which to present this conflict, and he turned to the new art form with surprising ease. His first draft, while in need of considerable reworking, was essentially the form in which the play developed.[23] The novelist had understood the demands of a theater audience and had avoided many of the digressions and diversions that had characterized his novels. However, it was clear that he would need further help, and it was at this point that Jouvet made his important contribution. Under the director's guidance, the new playwright learned the basic principles of his profession. He was taught to highlight salient traits of the characters and to develop the tensions among them, giving depth and authenticity. He learned about dramatic conflict and built up relationships among his characters. He was taught to tighten his plays so that the action could advance more quickly. Both men worked well together, and it was soon impossible to tell where the work of one left off and the other began.

The result of this collaboration was astonishing. The play that emerged was taut, logical, well-developed, and consistent in tone, virtually a *pièce bien faite* in the manner of Scribe.[24] The presentation of *Siegfried* on May 3, 1928, turned out to be an important moment in French theatrical history. The reviewers found the verbal creativity and the poetic vision a unique adventure in contemporary theater, although there was some criticism over what seemed to some Giraudoux's excessive admiration for Germany. The public accepted the play enthusiastically and the age of Giraudoux had begun.

Although the subject matter was basically the same as that of the novel, the differences between play and novel indicate that considerable changes were necessary. The novel was much more open and discussed the French and German cultures in greater detail. In the play, there are many references to the two countries, but the general discussions are secondary to the more personal drama taking place. In *My Friend from Limousin,* the author spent a great deal of time presenting his admiration for Old Germany and his dislike for Modern Germany, a theme much reduced in scope in *Siegfried.* On the other hand, many of the references to France are also eliminated, and the Limousin area, which had recalled Siegfried to France in the novel, disappears entirely. Giraudoux understood that the general public would not share the same sentimental relationship to the region that he did. Probably the most important change takes place in the central character. In the novel, the French narrator was essentially the main figure; in the play, he has disappeared, and the protagonist, Siegfried, has emerged from a nebulous, ambiguous characterization to become a clearly defined person, seeking his past in order to deal with his present. A significant part of the play deals with Siegfried's attempt to retain and merge the French and German cultures. As a result, the drama becomes more sharply focused and more theatrically effective.

Other changes occurred because of the need to make the characters from the novel function in theatrical form. Giraudoux's novels generally developed with seemingly separate, individual responses on the part of the characters, who rarely had any direct contact with one another. The theater, however, requires this contact, and a dramatist is obliged to establish relationships. Through Jouvet, Giraudoux soon saw this need and set up these relationships by means of scenes with two people in which each person presents his point of view, more in the form of a debate, however, than through realistic dialogue. Such a procedure allowed the author to make contact between his characters and, at the same time, to emphasize the ideas that the characters represented and that were still his major interest. When these changes were made, certain figures in the Giraudoux play took on new and expanded roles. Geneviève Prat had only a very small part in the novel. In the play, however, she is an important figure, and at times she receives almost as much attention as Siegfried. She now becomes a symbol of fidelity and compassion. When she hears that Jacques Forestier, her fiancé, may still be alive after being presumed dead in the war, she hurries to Siegfried, and her scenes with him, in which she convinces him of his need to return to France, are some of the most affecting of the drama.

Geneviève learns of Jacques's possible existence through Zelten, the impulsive German who had lived in Paris at one time. Zelten has also become a much stronger figure than in the novel, and in the play, Zelten and Siegfried are adversaries right from the beginning, establishing the necessary plot conflict. Zelten, still the poetic, imaginative spirit, opposes Siegfried because Siegfried represents a certain type of logic that has helped create an industrial, big business attitude that, in Zelten's opinion, is ruining Germany. He knows that Siegfried is Forestier, and in order to accomplish a *coup d'état,* he sends for Geneviève who, he hopes, will persuade Siegfried to return to France. Zelten's revolution fails, but, as in the novel, he reveals Siegfried's real identity. The struggle then begins in earnest for the soul and spirit of Siegfried, a struggle epitomized by Geneviève, the representative of the French *esprit,* and Eva, the German nurse who found Siegfried suffering from amnesia and who now urges him to remain true to his new land and life. Eva, who had been a fairly important character in the novel, is limited to a smaller role.

In the play, Siegfried is first called back to France not by the beauties of the Limousin area, as in the novel, but rather by his pet poodle, Black, who is waiting for him, a reference that may seem somewhat frivolous at first, but that actually alludes to Ulysses' dog in the *Odyssey* or to Tristan's dog.[25] In typical Giraudoux fashion, Geneviève poetically notes the other joys of life that will be awaiting Siegfried upon his return: his lamp, the initials on his stationery, the trees of his boulevard, his insects, his plants. In other words, Geneviève calls Siegfried back by means of the humble, simple things that make up his life. As she notes, this is not the time to consider the larger issues: "The greatness of Germany, the greatness of France, this is evidently a fine subject for antitheses and contrasts. That the two nations ... may have a different notion of good and evil, ... that is of course a good drama. But that, Jacques, that is the drama for tomorrow."[26]

A fourth and final act is added and takes place at the railroad station on the French-German border. The German side is neat and comfortable, while the French section is shabby and somewhat depressing. Siegfried has now made up his mind to return to France, but he hopes to be able to live with both the cultures that he has known, echoing once again Giraudoux's sentiments: "I will try to bear honorably the two names and the two existences which Fate has given me.... There are no sufferings so opposed, no experiences so antithetical that they cannot be merged one day into a single life, for the heart of man is still the most powerful melting pot" (*T* I, 64). And that possibility is reaffirmed at the end of the play when Geneviève, now sure of Siegfried's return to France and of his acceptance of his French name, dares to say to him: "Siegfried, I love you!" (*T* I, 72)[27]

For the most part, this first play immediately sets the pattern for the works to follow: Giraudoux sets up a conflict between two groups and looks for a synthesis of the two sides in order to create a better reality. In addition, the structure of *Siegfried* establishes the format for future works: an issue will be analyzed, debated, and dissected, generally by two characters. No conclusion will be reached, and a certain ambiguity remains at the end. However, in one respect, *Siegfried* is atypical of Giraudoux and of the type of theater that he would write. In this first play, Jouvet's influence was very important in helping the new dramatist create a work that would appeal to the general public. But it also seems to have somewhat diminished the Giraudoux spirit. As poetic and inventive as the play is, it lacks the sparkle and creativity that is found in his later dramas. Obviously, at this starting point in this theatrical career, Giraudoux did not feel sufficiently confident to use his fanciful imagination to any great extent. As a result, *Siegfried* remains a fine first entrance into the theater and, gauging from public reaction, a stunning success. Nevertheless, the quintessential Giraudoux style for the stage had not yet been fully developed. His next work, *Amphitryon 38,* was the type of play that the public would associate with the dramatist over the next sixteen years.

VII *Giraudoux and the Theater*

Once Giraudoux had made his sudden turn to the theater, he

soon developed very specific theories as to its importance and its place in society. In the years following his first successes, beginning as early as 1929, he started to establish an esthetics of the theater through a series of articles and lectures, culminating in the one act play, *L'Impromptu de Paris (The Impromptu of Paris)*[28] in 1937.

In these writings, the dramatist first points out the vital effect of theater on the public at large. In a period when people have more leisure time than ever, the theater is "the only form of moral and artistic education of a nation" (*OLD,* 574). It is the place where "the most humble and the least cultured public can be placed in personal contact with the deepest conflicts and create for themselves a lay religion, a liturgy and saints, feelings and passions" (*OLD,* 574). The theater has a dignity to it that far surpasses the ordinary. In fact, says Giraudoux, who always kept a healthy distance between himself and religion, the theater is like a religious event, and it is not by chance that, formerly, it was performed in or near churches. For, in a sense, drama is like a mass, and its function is to continue convincing those who are already convinced, the "faithful." Unlike the other art forms, theater is not meant to be avant-garde. Rather, it is a microcosm where all of the preexisting moral, sensual, and poetic feelings of the audience must find a place for expression. But, even though theater is not avant-garde, it must be at all times up to date, giving shape to the preoccupations of the spectators. Unfortunately, Giraudoux observes, the drama of the 1920s and 1930s gives the impression of belonging to another time, another period. It presents a series of false truths that reassure the audience but leave it uninspired and lacking in feeling.

The author maintains that part of the blame for this type of drama lies with the critics. On the one hand, they are much too indulgent toward mediocre or simply bad plays, and consequently, the theater has a poor reputation. On the other hand, the critics underestimate the intelligence of the public, and thinking that certain plays are too difficult for the audience, they tend to dismiss those works that have a feeling of "literature" about them, or, in a reference to Giraudoux's own type of writing, they reject plays that depend heavily upon language or dialogue. However, the dramatist contends, the public is more intelligent than the critics realize, and it is very willing to accept serious and demanding drama. In the final analysis (and here Giraudoux is once more speaking of his own theater), the public demands style: "Theater is not a theorem, but a spectacle, not a lesson, but a filter. Its purpose is less to enter into your mind than into your imagination and your senses and that is the reason, in my opinion, that writing talent is indispensable to it, for it is style which sends out a thousand reflections, a thousand iridescences over the souls of the spectators" (*T* II, 152). Since humans possess the gift of language, Giraudoux depends upon dialogue to reach the public: "The true *coup de théâtre* is not the noise of two hundred people, but the ironical nuance, the imperfect subjunctive or the litote" (*OLD,* 596).

In that respect, the dramatist feels that France is superior to a country like Germany, where the director has become so tyrannical. What is so important in Germany, he notes, are the stage, the sets, the mechanical devices. In this type of theater, Giraudoux is principally thinking of a director like Erwin Piscator,[29] while rejecting at the same time the Communism that Piscator represented.[30] In France, the scenic production is secondary to the text, to the word, which is king. As a result, the author plays a major role, and he in turn must give the public what it wants — imagination. The theater is not meant to be like André Antoine's *Théâtre Libre*[31] with its emphasis on realism, for example, placing a real clock with chimes on stage. The only moment when the theater becomes real, according to Giraudoux, is when the clock chimes 102 o'clock — that is, the theater is only real when it is unreal. The role of the imagination is foremost: "There are people who dream, but for those who do not dream, there remains the theater" (*OLD,* 574). Plays are not to be understood but to be felt. Imagination is the key element, and style is the means of expressing imagination.

Yet he understands that style is not alone in creating a piece of theater: "Theatrical life exists only by diversity. The world of inspiration must also be, like the real world, reborn each day" (*OLD,* 695). He sees improvisation as a major factor in the theatrical experience, and along these lines, he is aware of the importance of a good acting troupe in a play's development. He knows that his association with Jouvet and the actors of Jouvet's troupe inspired him enormously. At the same time, he is somewhat sad at the idea of a performance of one of his plays for, once that happens, the character in the work no longer belongs to the dramatist: "The first actor who plays him [the character] is the first in a series of reincarnations by which he becomes further and further removed from his author and finally disappears from him forever" (*OLD,* 709).

However, Giraudoux never loses his enthusiasm for the theater and for everything that it can do for the public. In fact, he even reaches the point of seeing the theater as an important factor in the running of the government, as he indicates in *The Impromptu of Paris*. The government should do all in its power to help the theater, says the Jouvet character in the play, since the theater provides so many benefits to people in dealing with their everyday lives. The Jouvet character observes somewhat ironically that it would be better for the government to illuminate a few brains than to illuminate the many monuments in Paris. For drama can provide the imagination that is the strength of a people, and it can prove to be an important force in society: "In this country, which has so many journalists and no press, which has freedom and so few free men, in which justice belongs a little less each day to the judges and a little more to the lawyers, what other voice remains than ours?" (*T* II, 165). Moreover, concludes the Jouvet character, if the theater is decayed, so, too, is the nation.

VIII   *The Gods Make Their Entrance:* Amphitryon 38

Some of these theories on the theater can be found in Giraudoux's next play, *Amphitryon 38*. In this imaginative work of great style, the dramatist created one of his most effective comedies. This time, he turned to a preexisting legend: the well-known tale of Jupiter (or Zeus in the Greek version), who seduces the beautiful Alcmene by assuming the form of her husband, Amphitryon, the Theban general. As Giraudoux's title, *Amphitryon 38,* humorously indicates, many dramatists had been attracted to this subject over the years, and this version is simply the thirty-eighth in line.

It appears that he wrote the play very quickly, perhaps as rapidly as three weeks, during the spring of 1929 when he was sick with influenza.[32] Giraudoux's *Amphitryon 38* has many similarities with the *Amphitryon* written by the dramatist Heinrich von Kleist, who, in turn, had adapted his work from the Molière play.[33] There is little doubt that Giraudoux was familiar with Kleist's work from his German studies,[34] and we have already seen that the title character of his novel and first play was called Siegfried von Kleist, the last name coming from the German writer. However, although he used Kleist as a model, the dramatist made the play very much his own, and it became the occasion for him to develop themes of deep concern to him: the feeling that the ideal, symbolized here for the first time by the gods and destiny, may be harmful to humanity; the possibility of humanity finding its own ideal within reality; the problem of the couple and the question of fidelity; and the value of a life lived by deceit.

In Giraudoux's version, the god Jupiter, accompanied by Mercury, arrives in Thebes planning to seduce Alcmene. They immediately begin their plans to create another war, so that the warrior Amphitryon, Alcmene's husband, will have to leave, and Jupiter, in the form of Amphitryon, will be able to spend the night with the beautiful woman. This plan succeeds, and the next day, Jupiter tries to tell Alcmene his real identity. However, she is unwilling to listen. In the meantime, Mercury has spread the story of the night to the people of Thebes, who are happy that the gods have so favored one among them. Nevertheless, Jupiter is still not satisfied, for he wants to be loved for himself, not because of his role as Amphitryon. He decides to return to Alcmene to reveal that he is a god. In this regard, Mercury tells her that Jupiter will be visiting her soon. Alcmene, in her turn, begins to devise her own plan. She receives a visit from Leda who, in legend, had previously been seduced by Jupiter when he had assumed the form of a swan. Alcmene begs Leda to pretend that she is Amphitryon's wife and play this role in the darkness of the bedroom. However, the real Amphitryon returns unexpectedly from the war, and in an ironic twist, Alcmene, believing that he is actually Jupiter, allows her husband to spend the night with Leda.

Jupiter still wants to possess Alcmene in his real identity. For her part, Alcmene persists in discouraging any romantic pursuit by cleverly offering the god something that he has never known before — friendship. She tells Jupiter that he will always be with her but in a different and better way: "First of all, I will think of you, instead of believing in you. . . . And this thought will be voluntary, coming from my feelings, while my belief was a habit, coming from my ancestors. . . . My prayers will no longer be prayers, but words" (*T* I, 165). Having understood her faithfulness and devotion to her husband as well as her need for purity, Jupiter relents as long as she can justify her refusal of him to her people. Alcmene replies that she will be glad to have the Thebans believe that Jupiter was her lover since she and Amphitryon know differently. Then, in a moment of doubt, she asks: "Are you sure that you have never entered my dreams, that you have never taken the form of Amphitryon?" (*T* I, 167). Jupiter lies, replying that he is sure, and Alcmene returns in her "pure" form to her husband.

Unlike *Siegfried, Amphitryon 38* falls more clearly into the pattern of the plays that the public would expect from the dramatist over the years. Giraudoux was obviously less restricted than before, and he gave more freedom to his poetic and whimsical imagination. The work, first presented on November 9, 1929, at the Comédie des Champs-Elysées in Paris, was an immediate success with the audience and ran for 236 performances.[35] While still following a basically straightforward presentation and structure, the play includes much more of the special Giraudoux style in its language, which some critics called *précieux*. Jupiter and Alcmene debate in witty dialogue that often sounds more like poetry than prose; there are frequent plays on words, anachronisms, and parodies of literary clichés; and paradoxes and antithetical statements are plentiful, providing a humorous framework for the comedy.

Like most of his works, *Amphitryon 38* is Giraudoux's attempt to find an equilibrium between the real and the ideal worlds. This time, however, he definitely sees the possibility of discovering the equilibrium within humanity itself, the ideal within the real. The central character is not a *jeune fille* like Suzanne or Juliette, but a mature woman who has come to terms with her life. Unlike Suzanne, Alcmene does not want an adventure with the unknown — and she says so repeatedly. Rather, she plans to find her ideal in her everyday existence. For a human being, "to become immortal is to betray" (*T* I, 129). Alcmene possesses the qualities of "the human infinite. Her life is a prism in which the common patrimony of the gods and of men — courage, love, passion — is changed into suitably human qualities — constancy, gentleness, devotion" (*T* I, 132). She has passed through the adolescent stage of the *jeune fille,* has found her role in the adult world, and represents a harmonious union of the ideal and the everyday reality. She symbolizes the synthesis of reality and the imagination found in the humble aspects of ordinary life, fully lived, the type of existence that Siegfried will follow upon his return to France, as will the controller in the later play, *Intermezzo.* Once again, this harmony recalls Giraudoux's retrospective look at his boyhood and his idyllic life at Bellac: "One can see quite easily that she [Alcmene] upholds a certain ideal of life and behavior which is, according to Giraudoux, that of provincial France. Alcmene's attitude toward the supernatural, her refusal to dream, her attachment to a private happiness deprived of tragedy can be found in Bellac."[36] In part, this sense of harmony carries over to another theme that would become increasingly important later on in Giraudoux's writings:

the couple and the question of marital happiness and conjugal fidelity. It is known that many of his female characters had certain traits in common with his wife, Suzanne, and at this particular point, Alcmene may typify the happiness that the author experienced in his own marriage, a happiness that would deteriorate as the years went by. Alcmene personifies all that is fine in the female: she is devoted to her husband and would rather die than deceive him. Her only guiles and ruses are directed against Jupiter, reinforcing the impression of her faithfulness.

However, there is a more troubled side to the playwright, and underneath the somewhat frivolous surface of the play, there are serious problems. As Pierre Brunel comments, Giraudoux was probably attracted to the legend of Amphitryon and Alcmene because it contained elements of tragedy as well as comedy.[37] The work, which basically revolves around a series of misunderstandings, makes one think of a play by Marivaux,[38] with whom Giraudoux has often been compared. But, the misunderstandings, while amusing, can also be of great concern, suggesting, as Claude-Edmonde Magny notes, "the impossibility confronting us of knowing the definitive truth about anything whatsoever."[39] We admire Alcmene and her witty replies to Jupiter when she manages to persuade him to leave her. Yet, in fact, she was seduced by Jupiter on his first visit. The seduction took place without her knowledge or consent, but it did occur, and in a strict sense, she has betrayed Amphitryon. In addition, she somehow senses that Jupiter did indeed possess her in the form of Amphitryon, and she questions him about this. The only way that she can continue to remain true to humanity and to her husband is to accept Jupiter's lies, which she does willingly, also asking that the god forget the whole matter. Thus, Alcmene's future happiness is dependent upon a deceit, a point which Giraudoux will explore in greater detail in his next work, *Judith,* and that will also be the basis of the very bitter and dark final play, *Duel of Angels.* Underneath the outwardly happy acceptance of life, there remains a conflict between purity and defilement with a subsequent resolution of the dispute through a covering up of the truth.

This same sense of seriousness underneath the comic element can also be found in the dramatist's treatment of the gods and of the role of destiny in man's life. For the first time, Giraudoux deals directly with the gods in his theater, and the writer takes special delight in showing their ridiculousness and incompetence on the human level. In one way, Alcmene triumphs over Jupiter, the master of the gods. He loves her and wants her to love him as a god. He fails because she convinces him otherwise. Alcmene is actually superior to the gods and rejects their authority: "I rejoice in the fact that I am a creature that the Gods have not foreseen... I do not sense a God who hovers above this joy, but rather only the free sky" (*T* I, 118). She is the liberated, unfettered spirit who defines the world of reality through her imagination. In this respect, she is clearly better than Jupiter and Mercury, who almost seem to be false gods with very little to do with the realm of the unknown, displaying a narrowness of spirit. Moreover, these "gods" are actually hostile to mankind. Just as Suzanne found nature on her island turning against her, so does Alcmene discover that the gods are planning her downfall. Nevertheless, as ridiculous as they may seem, they pose a great threat, for they are the agents of fate or destiny. In this role, these gods, instead of opening up the universe to mankind, impose the will of fatality. As clever and as intelligent as Alcmene has been, she has not been able to prevent what fate has had in store for her. She has been seduced by Jupiter and will bear a child, to be named Hercules. She has done everything possible to avoid her destiny and, yet, has not succeeded. Her triumph over the gods has not really been a triumph over fate. The only way she can regain some control of her life is to attempt not to understand what has taken place, to willingly deceive herself.

Even though these serious undertones in the play leave a certain ambiguity as to the author's intention, *Amphitryon 38* is basically an optimistic work, reflecting, for the most part, a happy view of life. But the seeds of discontent are present, and Giraudoux's Garden of Eden comes apart in his next drama.

IX   *The Spiritual Nihilism:* Aventures de Jérôme Bardini

In *Aventures de Jérôme Bardini (The Adventures of Jerome Bardini),* published in 1930, it is clear that the author was going through a critical period in his life. Although it contains some humor, the novel reflects more disenchantment than any other work of his up to that period, and the spiritual nihilism of the work comes through very sharply.[40] The previous indifference and the somewhat stoical outlook on life gives way to a strong desire to escape, to flee, suggesting that Giraudoux himself was having major difficulties in accepting his everyday existence.

The Adventures of Jerome Bardini is composed of three stories, the first of which had appeared as early as 1926. Although each story can be read separately, the character of Jerome Bardini and his quest provide the interlinking factors. In the first tale, "First Disappearance of Jerome Bardini," Jerome is overcome by the meaninglessness of life. Like Suzanne and Juliette, he longs for the unknown, for anything that will be able to change what fate has in store for him. Even though he has a child and an apparently happy relationship with his wife, Renée, the couple are only content on the surface. Jerome feels that his wife is not aware of the unrest in his soul, and he decides to take off on his own, leaving a note for his wife. Changing his mind, he returns for one last night, but finds Renée transformed. Jerome's comments reflect his own lack of appreciation of her situation: "This woman, who had never been anything other than tenderness, gentleness, modesty, looked at him with hatred.... He found Renée unjust. Women truly have the talent to take away from a drama or a difficult experience its generous quality and to send it back to you as a disloyal act.... The gentle and trusting being in Renée had fled along with Bardini" (*OR* II, 260). Renée tells him to leave the house, and his adventures begin.

In the second story, "Stephy," the action changes to New York, where Bardini has met Stephy Moeller in Central Park. In this work, the emphasis is shifted, with Bardini becoming a secondary, rather nebulous figure. Stephy takes over as the protagonist and assumes the qualities associated with the typical *jeune fille*. She, too, is trying to escape from her humdrum reality with her father, a music teacher, and with the two musicians who come to rehearse with him. Both of the musicians are pleasant but dull, and Stephy understands that one of them will one day be her husband. In the meantime, like all of Giraudoux's young girls, she does her best to avoid her destiny by seeking adventure, starting with her meeting Jerome in the park. She does not know his name, nor does she want to, for she prefers to think of him as *l'Ombre* (the ghost). Jerome is, of course, only a mere mortal, and he soon begins to lose much of his glamor for Stephy. He asks to marry her, and she is offended at the thought that their relationship requires the conventionality of a wedding. However, she relents and agrees to a marriage by a false priest, but she continues to lose interest in Jerome as her ideal becomes too real, and inevitably, she leaves him. In that respect, Stephy is simply following the path of all Giraudoux's adolescents as they move toward adulthood. Stephy returns to her father, and she will now accept her life with one of the two musicians. But such acceptance can only be accomplished with disappointment: "The two fiancés ... had already found a way of always seeing a joyful and agreeable Stephy, of always hearing Stephy laugh and sing. It was simply that they would never look at the true Stephy, bent and weary, never listen to her poor, tired words" (*OR* II, 306).

In the last story, "The Kid,"[41] Bardini finds a truly free person, seemingly in charge of his own destiny, but he loses him to the conventional forces of humanity. The Kid is a young boy who has lost his memory and has forgotten his name and family. When Jerome first spots him at Niagara Falls, he is overjoyed that, for the first time in years, he sees a being who does not seem an "accomplice" of humanity. In fact, the Kid's freedom is exactly what Jerome has been looking for: "An instinct of life so pure, a soul so free of the bonds that tie one from birth, that the word liberty takes on a new meaning when he is around" (*OR* II, 320). The Kid is close to nature, free from society's imposing laws. Although the boy is only twelve years old, Jerome becomes his disciple and considers him his god, his divinity. For the first time, Jerome reacts to another human being, but ironically enough, this human being is like a divinity, an almost too perfect ideal. In this way, Bardini is able to attach himself to something and transcend the spiritual nihilism from which he has been suffering.

Like all of Giraudoux's tales, however, this interlude with Eden ends in defeat. Mr. Dean, a representative of the school authorities, arrives to take the boy back to a "normal" life. Through a series of incidents, the Kid recovers his memory and returns to his family. Jerome is also recovered by his friend, Fontranges, who appears once again in one of Giraudoux's novels. Fontranges has come to America to take his friend, Bardini, back to France. On the return trip, an interesting conversation ensues in which Fontranges casts considerable doubt on the validity of Jerome's adventures. Fontranges asks Bardini if he does not feel that the source of his trouble comes from pride, that is, "a nausea about the idea of creation, a repulsion for our way of life, a flight from our dignities" (*OR* II, 338). In effect, Fontranges continues, Jerome developed an attachment for the Kid because he made no demands upon him. In a real family, and this is its blessing, Fontranges adds, demands are constantly being made. Basically, Jerome has never really committed himself to reality, and he lacks the inner substance that comes from such a commitment, perhaps a self-criticism on the novelist's part.

In one sense, Bardini's evasion of life is an expression of Giraudoux's disgust with reality and humanity. Bardini can see good only in the realm of the ideal, and like the Kid, he rejects humanity in order to arrive at this ideal. If this is so, Giraudoux was at his most pessimistic when writing these stories. Certainly, signs of this attitude are everywhere. Both Stephy and Jerome return to the mediocrity of everyday existence with heavy hearts and disgruntled spirits. Nor do they seem inclined to make the best of a less than perfect world. However, by separating Jerome so completely from humanity, Giraudoux probably wants to convince the reader (and himself) that Bardini has gone too far in his rejection: "The communion with the Cosmos is only a caricature if it is based on the refusal of communion with men."[42] Even while we may perceive that the Kid provides Jerome with a sense of direction in his own life, we also understand that the Kid's lesson is one of disgust with, and isolation from, humanity, a lesson that most people would instinctively reject. In the bizarre ending of the story, the young boy has fled the school authorities who want to take him back. Bardini finds that he has taken refuge in one of the power plants in Niagara Falls. Having passed out, the boy awakens to the sounds of iron, steel, and metal from the plant, all covering up the noises of humanity. If this cold and impersonal place is to represent the net effect of the Kid's flight from humanity, Giraudoux suggests, then there is small comfort to be found.

Inevitably, the final lesson of *The Adventures of Jerome Bardini* remains ambiguous, probably because Giraudoux himself had conflicting feelings. A pronounced disgust with humanity is present, and the author is desperately seeking some means of escape, indicating some sort of crisis in Giraudoux's existence. At the same time, however, the writer seems to realize that any total separation from humanity is foolish — or at least he will convince himself of that for the time being.

X   *The Defiance of the Gods:* Judith

Giraudoux's third play, *Judith,* continues the pessimistic outlook expressed in *The Adventures of Jerome Bardini.* Performed on November 4, 1931, at the Théâtre Pigalle in Paris, the play is a somber, bleak view of man faced with a repellent reality, with an indifferent God and with an all-powerful destiny. It is also a study of man's defiance of, and futile attempt to thwart, fate. It is Giraudoux's first attempt at tragedy, and he names it as such for the only time.

In essence, the playwright has taken most of the themes found in *Amphitryon 38.* However, in the earlier play, for the most part, the tone was light, bantering, and witty. In *Judith,* the dramatist is serious, bitter. What made him change at this point? Although there is no way of knowing for certain, it seems likely that the playwright was finding his personal life more and more difficult. When this play was first performed, Giraudoux had just turned forty-nine, was married, and had a child. The perennial adolescent had to face the fact that he was now middle aged. We know that his marriage became less and less satisfactory over the years, and it is reasonable to assume that he was experiencing some of the strains at that moment. Reality probably appeared increasingly unacceptable, and *Judith* is one of his first writings to express strongly his dark side, a side that would expand with the passing years.

Why did he choose the biblical tale of Judith? The writer may have been attracted to it because he had happened to chance upon the story so often in his readings. Albérès cites sixteen versions of *Judith* written by other authors, a list that Giraudoux had drawn up before writing his play.[43] In 1922, Henri Bernstein, a leading dramatist of the period, wrote a play on the topic, and undoubtedly Giraudoux knew something about the work. Jacques Body also makes a strong case for the version of *Judith* published by Friedrich Hebbel, a German writer relatively unknown in France, but whose play was first presented in Germany in 1840.[44]

Other sources also contributed to the work. Giraudoux has indicated in his book *Visitations* that the Austrian actress, Elizabeth Bergner, inspired him in the writing of the title character (*OLD,* 685). Miss Bergner had previously enchanted him with her performance of Alcmene when *Amphitryon 38* was presented in Germany. In addition, at this point in his professional career, Giraudoux held a relatively undemanding position on the Commission on the Assessment of Allied Damages in Turkey, putting him in contact with people from the Middle East. He probably was interested in placing on stage the people with whom he was dealing in his professional life.[45] We have already seen that Emmanuel Moïse, the Jewish banker, was an important character in *Eglantine.* And Jacques Body notes that, by means of the Judith tale, Giraudoux could attack Judaism and the Judeo-Christian tradition that the author rejected.[46] In writing this play, the writer could strike out at organized religion and its "gods."

In the biblical version, Judith is a widow in the city of Bethulia. A young, beautiful, rich woman, she has spent three years in prayer following the death of her husband. At the time, Holofernes, a general in the army of the Assyrian King Nebuchadnezzar, has invaded Bethulia and is attempting to conquer the Jews. Judith vows to save her city, and she pays a visit to the camp of Holofernes, telling him that she has important news. He receives her and is totally charmed by the seductive woman before him. After a banquet one night, when Holofernes drinks too much and has fallen into a stupor, Judith seizes his sword and cuts off his head, taking the head along with her on her return to Bethulia. Since the Assyrians are distraught following the death of their general, the Jews are able to defeat their opponents, and Judith becomes a heroine to her people for the rest of her life.

In Giraudoux's version, Judith is also a young, rich girl, but she has never been married. She loves to dance and to go to the theater and can seem at times a little silly, for she is among "the most frivolous, the most coquettish, the most changeable" of young girls (*T* I, 183). At the age of twenty, the supposedly virginal Judith is also very strong-minded and independent. The city of Bethulia is asking her to go to the enemy camp to kill Holofernes. Judith, however, is reluctant to go because of the absence of God: "I repeat to you that the voice of God is not for me. Ever since the city entrusted me with its safety, don't you think that I have tried to find a sign addressed to me by God?" (*T* I, 184). Like many of Giraudoux's main characters, she is waiting for a word, a "sign," this time from God. When Jean, her friend and a warrior for the Jews, tells her that everything is hopeless and that the Jews are likely to lose the battle, Judith suddenly changes her mind, refusing to accept the idea of defeat, and decides to go to the enemy camp. She is proud and stubborn whereas, in her mind, Jean and the people of Bethulia are weak. She will go kill Holofernes, not because God has asked it, but because she alone has decided to do so. Suzanne, a prostitute who resembles Judith physically, offers to go in her place so that Judith may preserve her purity. Judith rejects this offer, saying that she will use her purity to change defeat into victory.

When she reaches the Assyrian camp, a trick is played on her. In a scene reminiscent of George Bernard Shaw's *Saint Joan,* Judith is introduced to Egon, a homosexual in the camp, and is told that he is Holofernes. She allows herself to be kissed by Egon and is then mocked by the Assyrian soldiers who tell her that the whole incident was a joke. Holofernes appears and drives the others away. Giraudoux's Holofernes is a king and not at all the tyrant depicted in the biblical tale. He is a strong, confident, sensual man who identifies himself as "the worst enemy" of God, all of which attracts Judith. At this point, Judith sees her own people as weak and vacillating and the Assyrians as cruel and despicable. She feels abandoned and sullied by reality, and God has given her no sign of his existence. Amidst this degradation, Holofernes is exciting, forceful, even noble. Judith yields to his advances and gives herself to him.

In the third act, Jean and Suzanne come to Holofernes' camp intent upon assassinating the king, but they discover that Judith has already killed him. She acted out of love, not out of hatred;[47] she is happy that she made her own decision, she says, not one forced upon her by the gods. Joachim, the chief rabbi, realizes that the people of Bethulia will never accept this explanation, for they will be deprived of their desire to see God's will accomplished through Judith. The solution: Judith must pretend that she killed to fulfill God's will. At first, she refuses to play this role, but the drunken bodyguard of Holofernes convinces her that she has accomplished the very thing the gods — or destiny — planned for her. In spite of her rejection of God's will, she killed Holofernes, and she has acted out her fate. Realizing her defeat, Judith agrees to play the role — she will be a symbol, the people will have their idol, and, as she notes in the final, ironic line of the play: "Judith, the saint, is ready" (*T* I, 246).

Giraudoux has rarely presented reality in such an unappealing form as in this work. Judith is surrounded by a defeated people who use her as an object in their frenzy to triumph over the enemy. When she does agree and goes to the enemy camp, the Assyrians trick her with the homosexual Egon, an encounter that was viewed as a most sordid matter by the audiences of the 1930s.[48] Yet each time Giraudoux presents the unattractiveness of reality, he counterbalances this with the ideal. In this case, Holofernes represents the ideal, and Judith experiences the supreme joy of her escape from the real through her lovemaking with Holofernes. Like all of Giraudoux's heroines, she discovers that this paradise will not last

— she must leave to return to the everyday world. After their night of love, she realizes that he is still a human being and that her moment of perfection will soon be sullied with the sordidness of reality. By killing Holofernes, she is able to preserve that one moment of perfection. However, at the same time, she is also killing her own happiness. More than in the other writings up to this point, we sense the real tragedy of the conflict of the real and the ideal. Like Alcmene, Judith's return to reality entails playing a false character, pretending something that does not exist. Unlike Alcmene, Judith understands only too clearly what took place, and she suffers from the deception she must now perform. It is as if Judith (and Giraudoux) are telling us that it is extremely difficult being part of the human race. In effect, man must kill a part of himself in order to accept the responsibilities of the real world.

But the author is not simply commenting on the world of reality in the play. He is also attempting to deal with the realm of the gods. As Claude Roy points out, this is "the story of a young girl, alone, opposed to the world of the Gods — ... moving away from the will of God, i.e., Destiny — looking directly at him."[49] Like his heroine, Giraudoux would like to defy the gods, but he realizes that this is only partially possible because there are two types of gods. The first type has been created by reality — the gods in the minds of the people. Judith can never receive a message from them: "Not once since yesterday have I felt his touch or his presence. . . . I have had my God of childhood, my God of adolescence. If my God of puberty and adult life steals away, too bad for him. Ah! Joachim, I thought that I was insensitive to men. . . . But I am insensitive to God" (*T* I, 239). One of the major reasons that Judith is attracted to Holofernes is that he rejects these gods of the Judeo-Christian ethic. Moreover, their representatives, the rabbi and his followers, insist that Judith live a lie, that she spend a life of deception. Giraudoux refuses to accept these manmade "gods."

Nevertheless, there is a god whom the dramatist is obliged to accept: that of fate or destiny, the element that controls man and has total power over him. Recalling the protagonists of the Greek tragedies, Judith, the proud, the imperious, sets out to defy this fate or destiny, but she does not succeed. When the drunken bodyguard of Holofernes, the voice of reason, tells her that, in spite of all her efforts to avoid her destiny, Judith has nonetheless lived the legend the gods had planned for her, she realizes the truth of the statement and accepts her new role as "heroine" of the Jewish people with a mixture of indifference and despair; she is transformed, as Moraud mentions, into a "living dead," her revolt has become impotent.[50]

As in most of the plays by Giraudoux, the ending remains somewhat ambiguous. While Giraudoux reveals the sordidness of reality, at the same time, through the characters of Suzanne and Jean, he also gives evidence of the values of humanity and points out the pride and intransigency of Judith. It is possible to see Suzanne, the prostitute, and Jean, the warrior, as the real strengths of the human race (the first names are, of course, those of Giraudoux and his wife). They symbolize the dignity of humanity. Both characters try to prevent Judith from leaving for Holofernes' camp, and Suzanne offers to go in her place. Later, Suzanne sacrifices herself for Judith and dies claiming that she, not Judith, was the one who killed Holofernes. Suzanne's nobility contrasts with Judith's unyielding presence, and it is easy to feel that Judith, like the later figure of Electra, has been too rigorous, too demanding. Yet, in the final analysis, it seems more likely that Giraudoux felt a stronger sympathy for Judith. Both Suzanne and Jean have aspects in their characterization that are less admirable. There is a suggestion that many of Suzanne's actions are prompted by sexual impulses and are self-serving; Jean appears slightly weak and ineffectual. Judith's emotions certainly reflect more directly Giraudoux's reactions to reality, and her bitter appreciation of life most likely reveals much of the playwright's own feelings.

This serious side of the writer surprised the theatergoing public and the critics. *Judith* was very badly received by both groups, who had expected another *Amphitryon 38*. As a result, the play ran only forty-five performances. Time, however, has been kinder to the work, and over the years, it has emerged as a tragedy of considerable depth, indicating Giraudoux's strong sense of the tragic and his ability to transmit that sense theatrically.

XI The "Offshoot" Chapters: La France sentimentale

In 1932, a collection of eleven short stories appeared, many of which had been published earlier in various journals. In this volume, *La France sentimentale (Sentimental France),* Giraudoux grouped together stories dealing with the main characters from some of his previous novels — Fontranges, Dubardeau, Bardini, Bella, Simon, Anne. In most cases, these short tales are what Will

L. McLendon calls the "offshoot" chapters,[51] chapters that Girau-doux did not include in the novels for which they were intended. According to McLendon, Giraudoux often approached the writing of a novel without any precise idea about the shape or proportions that his narrative would assume.[52] He would sit down to compose with only a basic outline in his mind. Soon, his inspiration would lead him in a number of directions, he would try out an idea in one chapter, followed by a variation on it in another. As he progressed, he would realize that some of the chapters did not fit into the novel as it had taken shape. Since Giraudoux considered everything that he wrote in novelistic form as one long piece of writing, he felt that all of the chapters deserved publication in one form or another. *Sentimental France* includes a number of these "offshoot" chapters.

Most of the short stories in *Sentimental France* are moderately interesting, but they do not merit too much consideration. How-ever, three of the works reveal a great deal about Giraudoux's men-tal outlook at that time, and they may help to explain some of the personal anguish that he was experiencing. The author had now arrived at the middle period of his life, and there is reason to be-lieve, as we noted earlier, that this constituted a major crisis for him. Having experienced a lengthy adolescence, not having settled down until he was nearly forty, the question of age and the passing of time appear to have preoccupied him considerably.

One of the stories, "Ice Palace," deals with the topic of the gen-erations. The narrator, Philippe Dubardeau, last seen in *Bella,* is thirty-four years old and temporarily without companions of his own age. He attaches himself to a younger group of acquaintances, ten years his junior or more: "I was living once again with friends who had never seen death and had never made love" (*OR* II, 429). He learns their dances, their speech patterns. It is a rejuvenation for Dubardeau, but it is also a world in which he does not feel totally at ease. At the same time, he falls into the company of an-other group, this time people who are fifteen years older than he. Here again, he enjoys their company, although he is aware that their problems are different from his, for they are worried about the arrival of old age: "For two months ... I lived as a parasite with the younger generation, drinking stealthily of their youth, and with the older generation, I enjoyed a fruit not any the less forbid-den, and I was happy for, of these two ages, I did not have the ignorance of the first or the fear of the second" (*OR* II, 431).

Then, one day, Dubardeau meets both groups by chance at the same time, and he discovers that a father in one group and his son in the other both claim him as a friend. Dubardeau then turns to the elderly Fontranges for guidance. Here, his feeling of unease immediately disappears: "Lacking companions of my generation, it was not to be an older person or a younger person who were to give me the strength and the awareness of my age, but it was to be an old man" (*OR* II, 433). Fontranges gives Dubardeau a balance in his life, a sense of equilibrium, something that Giraudoux always sought desperately.

Two other short stories in this collection give further indications of problems in Giraudoux's outlook at that time. In "The Sign," the narrator hears that Dumas, a man whom he knew slightly during World War I, has just died in a swimming accident. At the beginning of the war, the narrator had drawn up a list of fifty of his acquaintances, including Dumas. Of this list, only thirteen people have survived. However, with Dumas's death, he forgets all the others and becomes totally preoccupied with this latest fatality. As has happened with the other deaths, the narrator looks for a "sign" from nature that will allow him to pass on to his everyday activities and forget the fatalities. However, he does not receive any sign and he turns away from nature in disgust. At this very moment, when he stops looking, he suddenly receives a sign and the story ends unexpectedly. A peculiar tale and not particularly good, "The Sign" is interesting only because it reflects a complete disharmony in the narrator's personality, and perhaps, by extension, in Giraudoux's. The narrator's obsession with Dumas's death indicates an almost pathological disturbance, and we are left to wonder if any of this was also present in Giraudoux himself.

The problem of obsession and psychological disorientation is raised in "Mirage of Bessines," in which the sense of mental anguish and disharmony is even more pronounced. Rémy Grand, a painter, is suddenly overcome with the vision of the small town where he used to live, Bessines, the same village where Giraudoux had lived briefly as a child. No matter what Rémy does or where he goes, he cannot escape the hallucination of Bessines, "the only town in which Rémy had never told a lie and [which] he had left at the age of eleven without any impurity. Only in Bessines had he believed without reservation in God and in all the saints" (*OR* II, 414). But he now begins to feel that there is something wrong in his remembrances of his childhood days. Rémy describes himself at one point as being taken over by the demon neurasthenia, the first time that this has happened to him in his fifty years (the same age as Giraudoux at the time of publication). He turns to doctors, but does not receive any help. He even begins to experience feelings of guilt about his past life, and he accuses himself: "Why did you never dare take your father in your arms, look at him and embrace him? ... Why does the death of a friend or a beloved relative cause you sorrow infinitely more violent than any other, but why do you experience at the same time a feeling of liberation, free of the weight of a great affection" (*OR* II, 420–21). Rémy's solution to the problem is to return to Bessines to try to find out what has been haunting him. A first trip back fails but, on his second visit, he finds a simple, humble village, full of ordinary activities that could not in any way be harmful. In effect, he has cured himself of his obsession, and he launches an attack on psychiatrists in general and on the Freudian school of psychiatry in particular: "To hell with psychology, and physiology, and psychophysiology. And to hell with Sigmund Freud. I pity him infinitely for having an evil tongue.... And to hell with psychiatry!" (*OR* II, 425).

This extremely violent reaction against the Freudian school of psychiatry is curious, especially in view of the fact that it comes from a writer who, at all other times, behaved with such discretion and moderation. It is possible that Giraudoux may simply have been reflecting attitudes of other writers of the time who were attacking Freud. But it also seems very probable that Freud's theories on childhood and its influences on man in his adult life may have bothered the writer who was so attached to his small town of Bellac. And Giraudoux's strong rejection of Freud may also represent an unwillingness to come to grips with his own situation, as he justifies himself by attacking that which he fears.

While we should avoid the temptation to search for exact parallels between Giraudoux and the characters in his stories, enough comparisons exist to suggest that the writer's world was becoming more and more complex, and his works were beginning to reflect clearly his dissatisfaction.

XII   *The Quintessential Giraudoux:* Intermezzo

Intermezzo, Giraudoux's fourth play, is probably his most typical and characteristic work. First performed on February 27, 1933, at the Comédie des Champs-Elysées in Paris, the comedy was immediately hailed by the critics and had a lengthy run. Since that time, *Intermezzo* has been successfully revived in France, particularly in a 1955 production by Jean-Louis Barrault, and has been presented throughout the world, including in the United States in Maurice Valency's 1950 adaptation titled *The Enchanted.*

In the play, Giraudoux generally controlled the darker side of his personality and presented to his public the wit and charm that was expected. Basically, *Intermezzo* is a comedy-fantasy directed to the imagination, a piece asking the spectator to suspend realistic interpretation and to follow the fanciful outlook of the dramatist. It is inventive and creative and soars beyond the ordinary to a fairy tale land. This is supposedly the first play that the dramatist developed from his own inspiration and whose plot was not dependent upon already existing sources or legends. According to Giraudoux's statement, which may be open to question, the original idea came from a 1577 painting that he owned, showing a group of actors about to perform in the *commedia dell'arte* style.[53] In the play, although Giraudoux retained some of the spirit of the *commedia dell'arte,* he once again drew most of his inspiration from the two sources that form the basis of the greater part of his writings: Germany and France. His readings in the German Romantic writers are clearly a major influence on the composition of the play. Recent studies by Colette Weil and Jacques Body have shown in considerable detail that Giraudoux's play, with its *état poétique,* has a strong kinship with any number of German writers.[54] Body, in particular, makes an interesting comparison between *Intermezzo* and Goethe's *Faust,* which he sees as a special inspiration to the dramatist.[55] Although the title, *Intermezzo,* may have come from sixteenth century Italy, where it was used to describe musical interludes performed between the acts of a serious drama or opera, it, too, could have had German sources, including Goethe and Heine.[56]

However, in the final analysis, there is no doubt that France itself, in the form of the small town of Bellac and its people, also served as a source of the play, perhaps the major source. The description of village life reflects an existence that Giraudoux knew well in his youth and to which he often returned in his adult years. And the theme of the play — the young girl's momentary flight to the unknown as an adolescent before settling down to an imaginative reality as an adult — recalls Giraudoux's novels of the early

1920s. Although he did not draw from classical mythology or legend for this story, the dramatist did use his own personal mythology. The story of Isabelle, the *jeune fille* and protagonist, is another variation on *Suzanne and the Pacific* and *Juliette in the Land of Men*.

In a small town in the Limousin region, everything has been turned topsy-turvy. A supernatural power seems to have taken hold, and strange incidents have been occurring: no one voted in the last election; women are leaving their drunken husbands for younger, handsome men; Monsieur Dumas, the town millionaire, did not win the monthly lottery as usual, but the poorest person in town won; the mother superior of the convent did not win the motorcycle as usual, but a young man interested in the sport of motorcycling won.

The person responsible for all of this is thought to be Isabelle, the young schoolteacher. She has brought to her profession a new and somewhat unorthodox approach. Rather than have her students learn their lessons by rote or memorization, she tries to teach them life's values through the use of nature. When an inspector arrives to check into the aberrations in the little town, he immediately questions Isabelle and her schoolchildren. He fails to grasp her methods and resents her school of the open air in which there are no doors, where the grade of zero is considered the best because of its resemblance to the infinite and in which there are no firsts or seconds among the students. But Isabelle is also suspect because each night she has been meeting a pale, handsome man who may be a ghost. To Isabelle, at any rate, he represents a romantic, idealized version of life: he has the attraction of the unknown, and she gladly rushes to meet him. To the inspector, the "ghost" is more likely the stranger who rented a chateau recently, then killed his wife and her friend and supposedly drowned afterwards. The inspector will prove that this is the reality of the situation, he says, and at the same time, he hopes to undo the strange spell that Isabelle or her friend has cast over the town. To do so, he hires two "executioners" who shoot the specter when he next appears to Isabelle. At this point, however, the ghost, who may have been a living human being,[57] becomes a true spirit, and he plans to return to meet Isabelle. She in turn is entranced with the possibility of a union between man and the universe, and she looks forward to her next contact with the specter — this time as a true spirit.

In the meantime, though, she has become interested in the controller of weights and measures, who stands for everything solid and substantial in provincial life. His love for her touches Isabelle, and at the moment that the ghost comes to take her to join him in his extraterrestrial universe, she reveals her affections for the controller by calling out his first name, Robert. The specter leaves her, for she has betrayed his world and has expressed her concern for reality, that is, she has passed from the time of adolescence into the world of the mature adult who accepts reality. In doing so, Isabelle faints, but a cacophony of sounds from the townspeople, recalling the joys of everyday reality, brings her back to her life with the controller. The village is now back in order, and we are told, with typical Giraudoux irony, that the millionaire, Monsieur Dumas, has won the lottery, and a legless cripple has won the bicycle.

For the first time in his dramatic work, Giraudoux establishes the young girl as heroine.[58] Isabelle is the perfect choice to mediate between the world of the routine daily existence and the creative realm of the imagination. As the druggist, Giraudoux's spokesman in the play, indicates, she is in the time of life when next to any other human being or any object, "she is the key destined to make everything understood" (*T* I, 254). During her youth, she was held back from the fascination of the unknown by her upbringing and schooling: "In order to obey my teachers, I insisted on refusing any other invitations than those of this world. All that they taught me, my schoolmates and me, is that this is a civilization of selfish people" (*T* I, 284). Now, she actively seeks the ideal, entering into a cosmic order where poetry and truth exist. More than any other person, the young girl has an affinity with the unknown. "Do you know of any encounter with a Ghost without a young girl?" asks the druggist. "It is simply that there is no other age which leads naturally to death" (*T* I, 304). The specter promises to tell Isabelle about the beyond; he will fulfill her fondest dreams. "Don't you see," she cries out, "that this visitor brings me what I have spent my childhood hoping for, a secret?" (*T* I, 311).

However, while Giraudoux (via Isabelle) may hope for a direct communication with the mysterious forces of the unknown, he understands, somewhat regretfully, that such a union is not possible. Although he may pose a problem that deals with the non-human, the dramatist realizes that the final answer to the problem lies within man himself. Thus, Isabelle is to find her fulfillment in her life with the controller, who has uncovered a world of the imagination within his own existence — he has discovered the poetry in everyday living. What he has to offer Isabelle is the wealth of life itself, full of warmth and delightful trivialities. In his occupation, he has found a way to enrich the process of living: "Each evening, when the sun sets and when I come back from my rounds, all I have to do is to dress up the countryside with the vocabulary of the Controllers of the Middle Ages" (*T* I, 307). Through his imagination, his town becomes one of those villages pillaged during the religious wars, and he becomes a German foot soldier. In such a way, the controller makes himself aware of the uniqueness of his life, and the world becomes a storehouse of the unexpected and unforeseen. By envisioning his future, whether in the small town of Gap or in the city of Paris, he meditates upon the real pleasures of existence — the beauty of a fir tree, the trotting races, the harvest season, the theater. His own creativity provides such poetry to these pleasures that life assumes a special meaning for him. This is Giraudoux's compromise. While the dramatist may be somewhat disappointed, for the moment he accepts the idea that man, living according to his nature, need have no regrets. The small, humble life lived completely is the answer to man's desire for that which surpasses him. If the fullness of existence is exploited, poetry, the unknown, and death will merely be a part of the natural course of events.

Intermezzo is one of Giraudoux's best plays. Under Louis Jouvet's guidance, the comedy possesses a structure that is one of the most solid of any of his theater. While developing a whimsical, fantastic motif, the dramatist created a "well made" plot that in no way encumbers the lightness and airiness of the work. If anything, the structure of the piece provides an effective counterbalance to what might otherwise be an elusive subject. Moreover, the scenes are carefully arranged to establish a contrast between the imaginative domain of Isabelle and the lifeless reality of the inspector or to highlight the differences between the ethereal realm of the specter and the warm reality of the controller. The author sets the play up around these distinctions, and the best scenes in the play occur when two characters, representing opposing points of view, confront each other. As a result, the vast majority of the scenes are so planned that their essential composition is a two character debate. In addition, with this comedy, Giraudoux displays new authority in his stagecraft, and by means of the druggist, he takes the audience into his confidence, indicating in an amusing way how he makes the transition between scenes. Throughout the comedy, Giraudoux never lets the spectator forget that his is a witty, ironic mind. Usually, the writer observes life's happenings with a wry, detached view — always skeptical, continually bemused. At times, his humor is expressed by physical acts as, for example, when the inspector defies the spirits, and his hat blows off his head. Yet, Giraudoux does not allow this type of comedy to overshadow the humor of his dialogue. Most often, he prefers the witty remark, the incongruous or unexpected observation, the clever or subtle turn of phrase.

However, even in this, the "happiest" of the Giraudoux plays, we sense an undercurrent of distress. After the ghost has been killed by the executioners, the druggist begs Isabelle's pardon: "For the fact that the ordinary people are always right, that only the myopic eyes can see clearly, that there are bodies and not ghosts.... That the world is not worthy of you, that it offers with generosity only its cruelty and its stupidity; that the Inspector is right" (*T* I, 296). And, even though the inspector is a figure of ridicule in the play, we nonetheless feel that Giraudoux places some of his own somber thoughts in his speeches. Probably paralleling the dramatist at his darkest moment, the inspector tells Isabelle's students what life is like: "A lamentable adventure with, for men, miserable beginning salaries, promotions at a turtle's pace, nonexistent retirements.... God did not foresee any happiness for his creatures: he foresaw only compensation: fishing, love and senility" (*T* I, 269–70). Even the young girl is a person who disappoints. When the ghost realizes that Isabelle will leave him for the controller, he tells her what her future life will be like: "And gluttony begins. And jealousy.... And vengeance. And indifference.... Goodbye, Isabelle. Your Controller is right.... You don't care about knowing something, you prefer to sway between two truths or two lies" (*T* I, 313).

From this point on, Giraudoux himself seemed to be writing as if he were swaying between "two truths or two lies." His works ranged from a seemingly contented view of man and his condition to the more tragic and pessimistic attitude previously expressed in *Judith*. Yet in spite of its undertones, *Intermezzo* is one of the dramatist's optimistic plays, the type most associated with him. The work's upbeat spirit, its fond recollection of Bellac and Giraudoux's childhood, and its sparkling humor represent the quintessential Giraudoux or at least the attitude that Giraudoux liked to present to the public and that the public accepted willingly.

XIII   *The English Adaptation:* Tessa

Tessa, Giraudoux's next work, is an adaptation of *The Constant Nymph,* a play by Margaret Kennedy and Basil Dean, based upon Miss Kennedy's novel of the same name. Presented on November 14, 1934, at the Théâtre Louis Jouvet in Paris, the work was quite successful and played several months. Although it had previously been popular on the stage in London and New York in its original version, at first glance it is a little difficult to understand why Giraudoux would have chosen to adapt this rather minor work. The adaptation was originally Jouvet's idea, and he encouraged Giraudoux to undertake it.[59] Once having started, the playwright remained fairly faithful to the original version, although he changed a few scenes and added some of his typical wit and humor. For the most part, the dialogue in *Tessa* is restrained and moderate, far from the usual Giraudoux verbal badinage. If nothing else, the adaptation indicates that the dramatist was capable of writing in a traditional manner, if need be. Ironically, the public responded favorably to the simple plot line and the more conventional presentation of characters.

The story of *Tessa,* however, does provide some clues as to the attraction it may have held for Giraudoux. The play begins in a country chalet in Tyrol in the house of a well-known English musician, Sanger. Sanger lives there with his third wife and his five children from previous marriages. The children, including Tessa, are all intelligent, witty, and outspoken and live in a state of pleasant anarchy. A number of guests are also staying in the chalet, including the composer, Lewis Dodd. However, the household has its problems: Sanger is an alcoholic, and the first part ends with his death. The younger children are now orphans (the third wife leaves after her husband's death), and their maternal uncle, Charles Churchill, and his daughter, Florence, arrive and plan to place them in a school in London. The plot takes a new turn when Lewis Dodd falls in love with Florence and plans to marry her. Young Tessa is very upset because she has secretly been in love with Dodd all along.

The scene changes to London, where Lewis and Florence are living. Lewis is unhappy in his marriage: Florence has tried to turn his career into a social event, and he is distressed. Tessa leaves her school, meets Lewis, and Florence wrongly suspects them of having an affair. She confronts Tessa and Lewis, and as a result, the two are thrown together. They realize their love for each other and flee

to Belgium. Lewis is willing to leave his wife: he has always toler-
ated her but never loved her. However, Tessa, always in delicate
health, is not able to withstand the emotional and physical strain
of their departure for Belgium, and she dies.

A closer look at the characters and situations in the play gives us
a better idea of what Giraudoux saw in it. In many ways, Tessa is a
sister of Isabelle or Suzanne or, in a later play, Ondine. She and the
other Sanger children are struggling, like the other Giraudoux protagonists, "to remain faithful to their natural harmony and to their
ideal in spite of the attacks of the debased world which surrounds
them."⁶⁰ Tessa seeks her ideal, her perfection, and she finds it in
her life with Lewis. But, she cannot sustain her happiness, and she
dies, setting a pattern for many of the future Giraudoux heroines
who would often face an unhappy end. In addition, Giraudoux was
becoming increasingly preoccupied with the problems of the
couple. Lewis and Florence are mismatched from the beginning,
and their marriage has never been happy. Each wants something
different from life, and the two can never find a common ground
on which to build the marriage. This type of unhappy relationship
would also become a constant theme in the forthcoming works of
the writer.

XIV   *The Crisis Continues:* Combat avec l'ange

Although *Intermezzo* was a refreshingly happy interlude in
Giraudoux's writings, in the 1934 novel *Combat avec l'ange (Struggle with the Angel),* the author once again deals with a moment of
crisis and a feeling of dislocation with reality, themes that were
treated in some of the short stories of *Sentimental France.* In
Struggle with the Angel, the main character is a person with rather
pronounced psychological disturbances, and the story centers on
the protagonist's effort to learn to accept happiness.

Malena Paz has supposedly led a completely happy existence: she
is wealthy, has a life of ease, but she feels guilty about her good fortune to the point that she needs to experience the unhappiness that
is known by the rest of humanity. As she says to her friend Nancy:
"I am afraid of being outside of life" (*OR* II, 512). The specific
incident that provokes her feeling of crisis occurs one day when, by
chance, she sees her lover, Jacques Blisson, walking down the other
side of the street. Upon seeing him, Malena understands that
Jacques has been thinking of her but, in his thoughts, he has

created an idealized, too perfect image of her that her real self can never equal. She feels inferior, and from that moment on, she questions reality, finally coming to the conclusion that she has never known the full variety of life. Malena asks Nancy to show her what the world has to offer in terms of reality; she wants to see misery, suffering, and death at close range. Once having accomplished this, she is still not satisfied and looks for further examples of suffering, showing signs of a pathological need for unhappiness. She finally ends up by convincing herself that Jacques has been unfaithful to her. In her neurotic state, Malena arranges to have Jacques and Gladys, a friend of hers, left alone in two adjoining hotel rooms. Nothing happens between the two since, in spite of Malena's forebodings, Jacques has always remained faithful to her. In the meantime, in despair, Malena has run off with the diplomat Carlos Pio, who has long been attracted to her. Jacques follows the couple and rescues Malena from the diplomat. At this point, the plot becomes even more involved, with Giraudoux giving full range to his extravagant imagination. Upon being taken back by Jacques, Malena faints. When she regains consciousness, she recounts a strange tale of being engaged in a desperate struggle with an "angel." Although she does not grasp the meaning of the dream, it later becomes apparent that the angel has been sent by her unconscious to tell her to be happy, to accept her life as it is, and to stop torturing herself with recriminations and doubts.

The most astonishing aspect of the novel is the central character, Malena, who has a definite psychological disturbance and pathological obsession. She is so different from the previous Giraudoux heroines, the *jeunes filles,* that it seems likely that the novelist was drawing upon recent experiences in his own life, on perhaps in his family, for his subject matter. The problems in his marriage were beginning to trouble him greatly,[61] and the difficulties of the male-female relationship now appeared with increasing frequency in his writings. Malena and Jacques had at first seemed like the perfect couple. However, when she becomes aware of his idealized image of her and of her own romanticized vision of him, she realizes reality's inadequacy. Man in his everyday existence can never live up to the ideal that he can create in his mind. But, rather than accepting this situation and doing what she can with it, Malena becomes obsessed with the idea of the perfect couple, trying to put Jacques and Gladys together, while at the same time suffering terrible attacks of jealousy, an indication of Giraudoux's increasingly pessimistic attitude regarding the possibility of happiness for the couple.

Along with the story of Malena, Giraudoux included an alternating plot line in the novel, and the two narratives together make a very curious combination. This second story allows him to deal with the diplomatic milieu, a subject that he had presented in *Bella,* and to treat another theme of growing interest, the question of war and peace. In describing the diplomatic world, which he knew so well, the novelist was able once again to satirize its bureaucratic foibles. He was also able to present a serious picture of Europe in the early 1930s, when the Western European countries were struggling with the possibility of war and the very real threat of financial disorder.

In this second tale, Jacques, Malena's lover, is the secretary of Brossard, the prime minister of France. Brossard is very clearly modeled on Aristide Briand (1862–1932), the French statesman who was premier of France several times and who was one of the outstanding advocates of peace.[62] Briand had been one of the supporters of Berthelot, whom Giraudoux portrayed in *Bella.* In *Struggle with the Angel,* the Briand character, Brossard, has actively sought to end war and to promote peace. However, he is now dying and has only a short time to live. One day, when he has fainted following an attack, he awakens to discover Malena at his side (she has come to see Jacques for the first time in his office). In an unusual twist in the story, Brossard associates Malena with the cause of peace, and later, when he is about to die, he asks for her. She returns to him and tells him, in a series of white lies, that the world no longer likes war and that happiness abounds, thereby making his death easier. At the same time, she finally rids herself of her morbidity over death, for she finds Brossard's passing both peaceful and beautiful. In this manner, Giraudoux combines the two plot lines with which he has been dealing.

This rather awkward merger of the two stories gives some indication of the weakness of the work. Giraudoux's loosely structured novels usually are successful because the writer's fanciful imagination has room in which to develop. However, at times, as in *Struggle with the Angel,* his imagination is too extravagant, destroying much of the reader's participation in the work. Nevertheless, the novel is of interest in the progression of Giraudoux's writings for it reveals that the author was finding reality increasingly difficult and that his world was in crisis. His future work would emphasize this new direction.

CHAPTER 4

The Final Years (1935–1944)

I N the last phase of his writing, Giraudoux became keenly aware of the fact that many of his earlier hopes had been shattered. At this particular time in his life (between the ages of fifty-three and sixty-one), he was well into his middle years and able to take stock of what had happened to him and of what he had accomplished.

From his beginning years, his most cherished dream had been the desire to transcend reality, to go beyond the humdrum disappointment of everyday living. In his previous writings, he had used the flight to the unknown as a means of escape, a way of finding an existence filled with imagination and poetry. Although he eventually settled for a poetry to be found in reality, merging the ideal with the real, the idea of a union with the universe always remained an essential part of his thinking. However, in this third phase of his writing, Giraudoux began to turn away from his basic theme, for he felt that it was no longer possible to find an accommodation with the unknown. What had once been attractive and exciting was now beginning to seem hostile. The unknown had taken on the form of destiny, controlling man's existence and seemingly leaving him no freedom. And destiny was seen for what it really was — an accelerated form of the passage of time. For Giraudoux the middle-aged man, time had begun to treat him badly.

One theme that had originally embodied many of his aspirations was the possibility of a merger of the best of the French and German qualities, the joining of the real and the ideal, the mixture of the solid and the instinctive. Reality was now beginning to prove how impossible that dream was. France and Germany were moving more closely to war with each passing day, and when the conflict finally did arrive, it simply confirmed the end of Giraudoux's hopes for understanding between the two countries. The symbol of France and Germany had been destroyed and with it all that it had meant on a personal level to the author. In his future writings, he

91

turned less and less often to German sources.

At the same time, reality found another means to defeat the author. He became more and more concerned about the couple and about the possibility of a happy union between man and woman. If such a union could be achieved, he suggested, it might then be possible for the human race to accept its existence. The joining together of the different but complementary aspects of man and woman could represent a pre-Adamite state, a time of innocence. It would then be possible to think again in terms of the alliance of the real and the ideal. Once more, however, life conquered this hope. Giraudoux's marriage was not going well: in the last few years of his life, there was a kind of separation between the writer and his wife, and he moved out of the couple's apartment.

Such disappointments in reality affected his work. The pessimism that had begun to develop at the beginning of the 1930s increased as the decade continued. The sparkle and the wit that had characterized many of his successful earlier creations disappeared entirely in some of his writings. Giraudoux started to question certain values in more detail, returning to problems with which he had dealt before and that he had managed to resolve in a seemingly optimistic fashion. He asked himself again to what extent a person could lead a life based upon lies. Although *Amphitryon 38* had touched upon the problem, later works like *The Liar, Electra,* and *Duel of Angels* raised it more directly and less discreetly. In contrast, the author also began to wonder about another type of person, perhaps one like himself, who demands absolute truth, absolute justice, absolute purity. These people are, like Electra, *femmes à histoires;* they cause pain to others, they make life impossible. Yet, in this life of degradation and sordidness, their demands are not without some justification. It would appear that Giraudoux found one absolute, one means of purification — death. While he obviously never advocated suicide as a solution to the problems of reality, he used it as a symbolic way of transcending reality, of arriving at the ultimate resolution.

But it would be inaccurate to give the impression that the writer had adopted a totally bleak outlook on life. His personality was much more complex and his works reflect the complicated human being that he really was. In his personal life, we know that Giraudoux remained a witty, amusing conversationalist. Although he may have appeared a bit aloof, he was always courteous and friendly. In spite of the disappointments he had encountered, he was still able to enjoy much of what life offered — he had numerous acquaintances, traveled frequently as part of his diplomatic career, enjoyed family life with his son and also with his mother and brother, and wrote continuously, achieving considerable success in the theater. Although it appeared a little less frequently, the optimistic side of the writer continued to reoccur in this last part of his career in plays like *The Madwoman of Chaillot* or *The Apollo of Bellac.*

While reality may have destroyed many of his hopes, Giraudoux seems to have heeded the counsel he gave to many of his characters in his works: accept life and do with it what you can. In this last period of his writing, the author became more practical, his solutions to problems became more down to earth. He now took it upon himself to advise his fellow countrymen. When he realized that the union with the cosmos was no longer possible, he decided that man could control a good part of his own destiny and could be responsible for what happened to himself. *Tiger at the Gates* is really a message about the forthcoming war with Germany and a plea that mankind avert this conflict, that it avoid its "destiny" to the extent possible. As early as 1933, Giraudoux also began a series of newspaper and journal articles on the situation of the Frenchman and what was happening to the quality of his life. He developed an interest in the problems of the city and wrote about urban living in the future. In *The Madwoman of Chaillot,* he warned the public about the dangers of big business, which exploits the ordinary person and ruins the urban way of life.

Pessimist, optimist — Giraudoux was both. Taken as a whole, his final writings do not reflect any one mood to the exclusion of another. In that sense, they are not atypical of the writer, who was never given to extremes. In earlier writings, when he found more reason to be optimistic, his works nevertheless bore traces of his darker side. As time and reality closed in upon him, his pessimism became more pronounced, often triumphing over his optimism.

I   *The Turn Inward:* La Guerre de Troie n'aura pas lieu

While Giraudoux had been gaining a reputation as the foremost French dramatist of the 1930s, he was still being considered as a playwright of charming, but perhaps superficial, works. At first glance, and without further consideration, comedies like *Amphitryon 38* and *Intermezzo* could lend themselves to such an interpretation. His next play, *La Guerre de Troie n'aura pas lieu (Tiger at the Gates),*[1] left no doubt that Giraudoux was a major dramatist, capable of treating an important theme while still retaining his uniquely imaginative approach to literature.

Tiger at the Gates, first presented on November 21, 1935, at the Théâtre de l'Athénée in Paris, deals with an unfortunately eternal theme: war and peace. The writer hoped to demystify war, to destroy its legendary qualities, to denounce its lies. Giraudoux wrote a play of actuality, and an important change seemed to be taking place in his writing: he did not seek an accommodation with the unknown. Rather, he turned inward — that is, he turned to man to find whatever answer there might be. The benevolent universe of his past writings had now become a hostile element and man a victim of fate or of what might be called the unavoidable.

Although he tended to deny it,[2] the initial inspiration for the play undoubtedly came from Giraudoux's increasing preoccupation with the growing belligerence of Germany. The rise to power of Hitler and the country's rearmament were causing alarm in all of Western Europe, In 1925, in Locarno, France and Germany had signed a pact to keep peace, a pact that was now in the process of being destroyed. In 1934, King Alexander of Yugoslavia was assassinated in Marseilles, and unease over the future of Europe was spreading daily. The inevitability of war was clear, and *Tiger at the Gates* was the dramatist's call to everyone involved to recognize the situation and to do something about it. Giraudoux's reactions were obviously affected by his lifelong contacts with Germany, and in its own way, his play is a renewal of the French-German question that the writer had originally raised in *My Friend from Limousin* and *Siegfried.* Once again, the dramatist attempted to find a resolution to this conflict, so basic to his own personality.

In typical Giraudoux fashion, the playwright presents the issue of war and peace not in a modern setting, but rather by taking his characters from legend and literature, dealing with the topic by allusion. Homer's *The Iliad* is the first source of the work,[3] with one significant difference: *The Iliad* starts with the tenth year of the war, whereas *Tiger at the Gates* begins immediately preceding the conflict. In the legend, war breaks out because Helen, wife of Menelaus, king of Sparta, is carried off by Paris, the Trojan prince and the son of Priam and Hecuba. Outraged by this action, the Greeks undertake an expedition against the Trojans, who are destroyed in the attack. Hector, the principal Trojan warrior, is killed, and his wife, Andromache, is taken away into slavery.

In the Giraudoux play, the Greeks have sent an ambassador to ask for the return of Helen, who has become a symbol of their country, and the Trojans are awaiting the arrival of the emissary. As in Europe of the 1930s, everyone is wondering if war will occur or not. Hector has just returned from battle and has no desire to see another conflict take place. He and his wife, Andromache, represent the forces of peace, an ideal that seems unattainable. Hector himself is definitely aware of the difficulties of changing man's basic nature: "If all the mothers cut off the right index fingers of their sons, the armies of the universe will fight without index fingers.... And if they cut off the right legs of their sons, the armies will be one-legged.... And if they gouge out their eyes, the armies will be blind" (*T* I, 450). He has, moreover, some formidable enemies within his own ranks who are very willing to see another war break out: his father, King Priam, who represents the government; Demokos, the poet, the personification of the press; Busiris, a lawyer; and the whole mass of people for whom war has its own special attractions. For some, war is a means of trying to find a justification for their disappointing lives. For others, it is a scorn for life, a way of reaching out for immortality. In this respect, it is ironic that the people who are attracted to battle share many of the same sentiments as Isabelle or Suzanne, who also sought an ideal that would place them in contact with the immortal. However, Giraudoux now rejects any attempt to go beyond the human realm.

Hector will go to any length to avoid war; he even allows himself to be humiliated by one of the Greek representatives, who slaps him and whom he refuses to fight. Hector, the experienced warrior, knows what battle is really like, and when he is called upon to make a speech to the dead, supposedly honoring those who have died in battle, he tells the truth:

I want you to know that I do not have the same sympathy and respect for each one of you. Even though you may be dead, there is among you the same proportion of courageous and cowardly as there is among us who have survived, and simply because of a ceremony, you are not going to have me mix up the dead whom I admire with the dead whom I do not admire. But what I have to say to you today is that war seems to me the most sordid and the most hypocritical recipe for equalizing human beings and that I would not any more accept death as a punishment or as atonement for the cowardly person than I would accept it as a reward for the living. (*T* I, 485)

In this speech, Giraudoux, through Hector, takes great pleasure in satirizing the type of address given in every French town in which war is made to seem more attractive than peace. Later, Andromache contradicts Hector, perceptively pointing out that war actually takes away all the courageous men, because they are the ones who die in battle, whereas the cowards are those who have escaped death and remain alive.

Hector refuses to allow himself to be defeated by the odds against him. He manages to convince Priam and the old men in the town to renounce their concept of the beauty of war, and he also reduces the influence of Demokos, who is actively promoting a conflict. Hector is even lulled into thinking that he has managed to win Helen to his side. However, in her case, he has run up against a powerful opponent. Helen has become a symbol of the beauty of war, but she is a beauty without much heart or soul. What is most tragic about her abduction by Paris is that the incident has not been taken seriously by either of them. Unlike Hector and Andromache, who seem to represent Giraudoux's ideal of the perfect couple, Helen and Paris embody the worst qualities of the male-female relationship. Neither one is committed to the other, and at the beginning of the second act, Helen embraces young Troilus, a fifteen year old boy whom she meets, suggesting that she is perfectly able to pass with ease from one male to another. Because they toy with love, Paris and Helen are extremely dangerous — they are in the process of unleashing a tragic war. In an interesting comment, Andromache observes that she might even be able to accept everything that is going to occur if Paris and Helen truly loved one another — the dramatist here pointing out the awesome powers of a couple who have found love. In fact, continues Andromache, maybe the love of the young couple could possibly stop the effects of destiny: "No one, not even fate, dares attack passion with an easy heart. And even if the attack did take place, it wouldn't matter!" (*T* I, 489).

Clever and witty, Helen, the pretext of the war, is always one step ahead of the other characters. In fact, in her scenes with Hector, she is calm and controlled, while he is carried away and unable to restrain his emotions. In the final analysis, she is infinitely more perceptive. When Hector is trying to persuade her to return to Sparta in order to end the conflict, she agrees to do so, but she warns him that there is something or some element that far surpasses her decision. Hector may try to close the gates of Troy, thereby signifying peace, but in spite of all his efforts, the gates will reopen and war will come charging in.

The force of this unchangeable, unavoidable future, which may be called destiny or perhaps more accurately the ineluctable, becomes evident in the second act. With the arrival of Ulysses and his followers from Greece, the people of Troy are in a state of extreme excitement. Ulysses' reputation has preceded him, for he is a person of considerable intelligence and finesse, possessing a deep knowledge of men. Hector has already worked out an agreement providing for Helen's return to Greece. However, Ulysses will accept it only if he can be guaranteed that Helen has not been touched by Paris. Stung, the people of Troy cannot contain their indignation over this attack on their virility, and they soon tell in specific detail how Paris took Helen. Although the agreement has now been broken, Ulysses is willing to meet with Hector to discuss ways of avoiding the forthcoming conflict. With his experience and his years of dealing with people, he does not have many illusions about man's ability to thwart what is to take place. Disenchanted, sad, Ulysses immediately clarifies matters for the idealistic Hector: "You are young, Hector!... On the eve of every war, it always happens that the two leaders of the people in conflict meet alone in some harmless village, on the terrace at the edge of a lake.... And they agree that war is the worst scourge.... And they are really filled with peace, with desires for peace.... And the next day, nevertheless, war breaks out.... The privilege of the important people is that they can view the catastrophes from a terrace" (*T* I, 502–03).

Ulysses also knows that any incident, even insignificant, can provoke the conflict. But he is willing to try to deceive the fates. He agrees to leave with Helen, and hopefully, war will be avoided. Ulysses accepts this plan for another reason: he has observed that Andromache flutters her eyelids in the same way that his wife flutters hers. Here Giraudoux, the diplomat, who has seen statesmen at work at close quarters, shrewdly points out that important decisions in world affairs are often made for very superficial and trivial reasons.

Hector now happily foresees a future of peace, but the fates are ready to deal him the final blow. Just as Ulysses is leaving, Oiax, one of the Greek soldiers, appears in a drunken state and begins to make advances to Andromache. Even Hector becomes angry, but fortunately, Oiax is finally persuaded to leave, and once more, disaster has been averted. At that moment, however, Demokos arrives, filled with rage and planning to arouse the Trojans to fight before the Greeks have a chance to depart. In a desperate gesture, Hector stabs Demokos, announcing to Andromache that the Trojan War will not take place, as the curtain begins to descend. But the Trojans arrive, and the dying Demokos claims that Oiax, not Hector, has killed him. Hector is now powerless to stop the conflict, and the Trojan War will take place, the curtain rising once more.

In this final moment, Giraudoux has created the height of ironies: Hector, the advocate of peace, becomes the actual cause of the war. If he had not stabbed Demokos, it is likely that Demokos would have been unable to arouse the Trojans to fight. It is an even greater tragic irony that Hector probably would never have lost control and stabbed Demokos had he not been aroused to battle by Oiax's attempts to embrace Andromache. As a result, the "perfect" couple brings about the greatest destruction. Finally, the play ends with a touch of the absurd. When the gates, which have been closed, reopen, the last view that the audience has is of Helen kissing Troilus. This underscores the tragedy of a war being fought over someone like Helen, for whom love is nothing but a plaything. The ending also suggests that Helen was only an excuse for the battle that had to take place.

Tiger at the Gates has been one of the dramatist's most durable plays since it was first presented and may very well be the most popular with audiences of any generation. Spectators respond eagerly to the theme of war and peace, and the bitter irony of the French title, "The Trojan War Will Not Take Place," leaves its mark. It has been the custom to interpret the play as an indication of man's impotence when faced with an all-powerful destiny, and there is much in the work and in Giraudoux's writing to emphasize his concern with the unknown and its control over man.

However, *Tiger at the Gates* also seems to reflect a new direction on the part of the writer, a turning inward toward man and his responsibilities, away from the universe. At the very moment that the dramatist makes destiny one of the principal forces in his work, he also seems to be looking to man himself, trying to find in what way man can take over some of the direction of his life. Jacques Body has taken this position in his recent work,[4] and Giraudoux himself indicated this direction in an interview with Benjamin Crémieux. Crémieux had asked the playwright: "If war is due only to obscure human forces which unleash it against the will of the best people and the wishes of the humble, can we not conquer these forces?'' Giraudoux replied: ''I am attempting to name these obscure forces and to remove from them that which is obscure, to show them in full clarity. I am doing my job if I have convinced the people who listen to me to act against them, to break them.''[5] In this sense, Giraudoux seems to be placing the responsibility for war on mankind. Fate does indeed play a part, but there is much that can be done by humanity to deflect fate's intentions, to lessen the effects of its force. In effect, as Cassandra, the seer, notes in the play, destiny is simply the ''accelerated form of time'' (*T* I, 447). This ''destiny,'' this passage of time, is composed of human actions. If men will make an attempt to watch over their lives, fate may take a different direction. This was Giraudoux's plea to the people of his time. War with Germany seemed inevitable, but the dramatist felt that something could and should be done to prevent it. Man must assume the task.

II   *Nature and Civilization:* Supplément au voyage de Cook

Supplément au voyage de Cook (Supplement to Cook's Voyage) was presented as a curtain raiser to *Tiger at the Gates* on November 21, 1935, at the Théâtre de l'Athénée in Paris. Although the one act play is not of any great consequence, it is charming and provides a delightful framework for the typical Giraudoux wit and spirit. The subject of the play, the free and unrestricted life on a South Seas island, was a natural topic for the dramatist. In *Suzanne and the Pacific,* Giraudoux had already shown his interest in the concept of man leading a life free from the limitations of civilization. He probably turned to the subject again since, in his new position as inspector of the diplomatic and consular posts abroad, he was expecting to travel to the French colonies in the Pacific and in Southeast Asia.

The specific source for Giraudoux's play was the well-known work written by the eighteenth century philosopher, Denis Diderot, *Supplement to the Voyage of Bougainville* (1773). Diderot's study dealt with a trip made by Louis-Antoine de Bougainville in 1768. Bougainville, in charge of the frigate *La Boudeuse,* was traveling around the world when he made a stop in Tahiti, where he was most enthusiastically received. Once back in France, he recounted his impressions of Tahitian customs in his book *Voyage Around the*

World (1771). One of his most important contributions was the fact
that he indicated that the "natives" of Tahiti lived a healthy and
pleasant life, far removed from the corruption that civilization
brought to society. Thus, Bougainville helped support Rousseau's
theories about the basic natural goodness of man and its resultant
destruction through civilization. In Diderot's story, the writer
strongly criticized Bougainville for helping to corrupt the happy
people of Tahiti with his civilizing ways. In fact, however, Bougainville was a most enlightened navigator and did not make any
attempt to impose his way of life.

In Giraudoux's version, in order to provide a more suitable
antagonist, the dramatist replaced the character of Bougainville
with Captain James Cook,[6] who had dealt, sometimes unfairly,
with the island people. Captain Cook himself does not appear in
the play, but he is represented by a Mr. Samuel Banks, a taxider-
mist and a deacon of the church.[7] Mr. Banks embodies all the rigid-
ity, narrowmindedness, and pomposity that civilization can offer.
He has come to help the people on the island, and his words of
advice are ridiculous and self-serving. His role is very much like
that of the inspector in *Intermezzo,* for he treats the Tahitians like
children. At the same time, their naturalness and spontaneity
deflate the exaggerated self-importance of Mr. Banks. He is
shocked when Outourou, the leader of the island, offers the
Englishman his wife and/or daughter as a welcoming gift. Mr.
Banks is accompanied by his own wife, who shares her husband's
sense of morality. She, in turn, is scandalized when Outourou,
upon discovering that she is childless, offers one of his relatives
who would be willing to help her "make a child."

Mr. and Mrs. Banks have much more serious matters on their
minds. They are planning to provide the Tahitians with some sense
of what is necessary for every civilized society: work, property,
morality. However, once they have finished their lesson, Outourou
and his compatriots understand only that a spade should be used
for fanning oneself or for protecting oneself from the sun but never
for digging; that property comes about only by means of theft; that
young girls should bestow their favors upon their guests, during
which time the valuables of the guests can be stolen from them.
As Outourou notes: "This is the teaching which the skillful Mr.
Banks has given us in two hours. . . . Everyone may leave now! The
island is ready!" (*T* II, 128–29). Civilization has now made its ap-
pearance.

In this lighthearted work, Giraudoux deals once more with his version of an enchanted island, and he is able to poke fun at the restraints that civilized people normally impose upon themselves. Again, he places the couple and its problems under scrutiny. One of the Tahitian girls talks about marriage to Mrs. Banks, cleverly commenting on the separation between husband and wife:

TAHIRIRI: A wife is the one before whom the husband feels more noble, more handsome, stronger, the one whose view incites him ... to war. From the moment you entered, Mr. Banks became bent over, grew duller. No doubt about it, he feels less handsome.... Are you really his wife?
MRS. BANKS: For thirty years, and the only one!
TAHIRIRI: The only one for thirty years! The only one for eleven thousand nights! (*T* 11, 116)

In fact, like all the Giraudoux characters, Mr. and Mrs. Banks live their real lives in their dreams — they imagine the people who will really give them pleasure, and their idealized creations of love have nothing to do with the reality of each other. Mrs. Banks tells this to the son of Outourou, her ardent suitor: "I now only like invisible men. My unique joys come from them. Rather than the presence of Mr. Banks, however superb he is, I still prefer the absence of Mr. Banks. And I very much prefer, precisely because I like you, to place you for the rest of my life in the groups of friends whom one does not see. If I spend tonight with you, impossible. You will be nothing more than a body for me" (*T* II, 125). In other words, he can truly exist for her only in her dreams, her imagination. Even now, when reality is beginning to make major inroads into the works of Giraudoux, the writer, like his characters, can never abandon the joys of the unreal, the poetry of the unknown.

III   *The Unfinished Works:* La Menteuse *and* Les Gracques

Following *Tiger at the Gates,* Giraudoux did not publish any major novel or play during the year 1936, but wrote a series of articles for newspapers and journals. It could seem as if he had entered a less productive period in his career. Part of the reason for this hiatus was due to his duties as inspector general of diplomatic and consular posts abroad, which required him to travel extensively. But another reason was that, while he actually did do some writing during this period, it was not immediately published: a novel, which he finished but did not revise and which did not appear until after his death; and a play of which he wrote only one act.

Sometime between March and June 1936, while he was on a trip to North and Central Americas as part of his diplomatic duties, Giraudoux wrote the only "psychological" novel of his career, *La Menteuse (The Liar)*. Once having finished it, although he mentioned the work to his friends, he never attempted to publish it, possibly because, as his son notes, his father did not wish to reveal some personal experiences that made up the basis of the story.[8] As a result, he apparently had no desire to polish or perfect the novel, and it never reached the final stages of composition. Although a portion of the manuscript had existed for some time, the complete manuscript was missing until 1968 when a British scholar, Roy Prior, found it among the papers of the author. The work was subsequently published in its entirety in 1969.

The Liar is a psychological analysis of love told in a manner somewhat reminiscent of Marcel Proust. Giraudoux's new approach to the novel form is at first startling and intriguing. But the psychological analysis, while often subtle and perceptive, never really possesses the depth that one might expect, and the improbability of situation and characterization considerably lessens the overall effect. Moreover, it is soon apparent that the pattern of the novel is a return to that found in Giraudoux's middle period: the real-ideal conflict and the eventual compromise between the two sides. This time, though, following his pattern in the later phase of his writing, the ideal has nothing to do with the universe but refers directly to man.

Nelly, the heroine, is no longer the virginal young girl of earlier works; she is a woman who has been having an affair with Gaston, a middle-aged businessman. This affair is predictably dull, for Gaston has none of the imagination Nelly seeks. While he is a basically decent person, he has an earthly reality that leads her to look elsewhere. When Gaston is away on a business trip, she meets Reginald, who represents exactly what she has been seeking: the esthetic, the pure, the ideal. Interestingly enough, Reginald seems to be a counterpart of Giraudoux at a slightly earlier period in his life — he is a bachelor, forty years old, a diplomat, very elegant and refined. As a result, she is obliged to lie to him in order to retain his interest. Nelly tries to hide her background from Reginald, and she makes up a tale of her great wealth, mentioning a previous marriage to a man of high rank, thus maintaining her respectability. In order to please Gaston, Nelly has been assuming a different personality, becoming commonplace and ordinary. With the addition of Reginald as her lover, she has two separate characterizations to maintain, and she must now lie to both men. Inevitably, her schemes collapse, and the two men uncover her falsehoods. Nelly knows that she will lose Reginald, whom she would like to marry. Caught between this conflict of the real (Gaston) and the ideal (Reginald), Nelly meets the Baron de Fontranges, who reappears in yet another story and provides the compromise solution. Fontranges will marry her and take up the reality that Gaston represents. At the same time, since he is considerably older than she, there is a suggestion that their marriage will involve little, if any, sex, and the sense of purity she presented to Reginald will be retained.

At this point, Giraudoux adds an especially bizarre twist to the tale. Gaston loses his memory in an airplane accident, and he does not recall his relationship with Nelly, thinking that she is his cousin. Since he is unable to tell anyone about her past, she can return to Reginald. In the climactic scene, Fontranges asks Reginald to accept Nelly. As Giraudoux observes: "There had never been offered a more beautiful occasion for life to forget its destiny and to have a little imagination."⁹ Although he loves Nelly, Reginald is too much obsessed with the question of purity and perfection and cannot bring himself to accept her, now that she has revealed her impurity and lies.

Besides the conflict of the real and the ideal, Giraudoux also deals with the topic of purity and perfection and the question of leading a life based on lies, preoccupations he had had since writing *Amphitryon 38*. Nelly, Giraudoux's first attempt to create a full-bodied psychological character, is a woman who lives her life through lies. Her relationships, not only with her lovers but with her acquaintances, are founded upon deception, and most often, her actions are self-serving and scheming. At the same time, some of these lies have a more complex reasoning behind them. It seems, in part, as if Nelly invents stories in order to fulfill the images that her lovers have created for her. Moreover, her affairs with Gaston and Reginald represent her desires to escape a humdrum reality and "some of Nelly's lies appear to be imaginary projections of certain normal, and perhaps even fine, longings that are latent in her and have not received their fulfillment in her actual life. Thus a subconscious craving for motherhood and a nostalgic aspiration toward purity may be at least partly responsible for the patent falsehoods she told to Gaston and Reginald."[10]

Since the novel was inspired to some extent by the author's personal experiences, it is entirely possible to see a certain amount of self-criticism in the Giraudoux character, Reginald. Reginald is unable to accept his happiness with Nelly because he has an almost absurdly high standard of perfection. Is Giraudoux suggesting that he too may share some of the guilt in his personal relationship with his own "Nelly"? "Nelly" would be just one more disappointment in reality for the writer, one more part of living that failed to measure up to the high ideal he had set for it. The possible autobiographical elements of the novel are the most interesting parts for, in the final analysis, *The Liar* ranks among the less effective of the Giraudoux novels. Having attempted psychological characterizations, the author does not allow Nelly and the other figures to exist as independent creations — they embody too closely the novelist's specific ideas. Moreover, Nelly's almost neurotic condition is never clearly explained. Is she meant to be typical of a certain type of woman? Is she a specific individual case? What causes her to act in so bizarre a manner? These questions are no more answered here than in any of his other novels, which do not claim to be psychological works.

In mid-June 1936, even before he had finished writing *The Liar,* Giraudoux started work on the play *Les Gracques (The Gracchi).*[11] This was to be a tragedy, dealing with the subject of civil war. Only one act of the play has ever been found, although Louis Jouvet maintained that Giraudoux read two acts to him in 1942 (*OLD,* 795).

The play has much in common not only with *The Liar* but with *Electra,* which follows, for the theme again deals with purity and perfection. Caius Gracchus is awaiting the return of his brother Tiberius, a Roman general who has just triumphed in battle. In Caius's view, Tiberius has lost his sense of decency in the war and is now consumed only with his ambition to see Rome become the conqueror of all countries. Tiberius, maintains Caius, is convinced of his own purity and perfection and is unable to see the corruption that has overtaken Rome. Caius, therefore, plots against his brother, planning to wage a fratricidal war. At the end of the first act, the two brothers meet upon Tiberius's return. Caius, the revolutionary, questions his brother, the dutiful soldier, about his feelings when he sees a triumphant, happy Rome gloating over its military victories. Tiberius's response is: "I am ashamed" and Caius exclaims: "O Tiberius! You are my brother" (*OLD,* 794), indicating that, underneath, they share the same concept of, and desire for, purity.

The Gracchi continues the recent change in Giraudoux's writing. As Jacques Body points out, the political situation in the play is not international but rather reflects an internal, civil struggle.[12] In this respect, the play reflects the turn inward during this last part of Giraudoux's career. Not only have the gods and the universe disappeared, but the writer has turned his attention away from other nations, directing it instead to his fellow countrymen. As Caius says to his wife: "O Lavinia, there are periods when man discovers that his worst enemy is not the assassin, not the foreigner, but his fellow countrymen, his blood brother" (*OLD,* 779-80). Moreover, he now begins to understand the sense of all wars: "Every foreign war is only a brilliant means of escaping a civil war" (*OLD,* 780). Giraudoux would pick these ideas up again and use them in his next play, *Electra.*

IV *The Absolute and the Relative:* Electre

Near the end of 1936, Giraudoux finished his seventh major play, *Electre (Electra).* He wrote the work within a few months, continuing many of the themes with which he had dealt in *The Liar* and *The Gracchi.* Once again, the dramatist raises the issue of purity and perfection, along with the conflict of the absolute and the relative. The writer questions the extent to which one can require total justice, total truth, total purity. At the same time, he also considers the problem of compromise, wondering if man can lead his life based on a denial of the truth. These topics are not really new to Giraudoux, for they simply represent further reflections on ways of dealing with an imperfect reality, the basis of his work since the beginning. The major difference is found in the point of view now adopted by the author. Whereas earlier he had turned to the universe for answers, man has now become the center of interest. Although the gods are present in the play, they are not the forces that guide the fates, but rather man himself is responsible, as Lise Gauvin notes: "Man participates more and more in his own destiny to the point that he becomes, in the absence of the Gods, the very incarnation of this implacable fate."[13]

As he turned the range of his vision inward, Giraudoux stopped using the French-German differences as the symbol of his concerns.[14] He now directed his attention to the problems within France, that, politically and economically, had been going through a period of extreme unrest. In 1936, the country had elected a Popular Front government composed of Socialists and Radical Socialists with the Communists on the fringe but wielding a certain influence. Surrounded in Europe by fascist governments, either present or imminent, in Italy, Germany, and Spain, France was marked by internal dissension, and Giraudoux felt the need to deal with the immediate and dangerous reality in his country.

Nevertheless, the writer still used his own terms in approaching reality. He turned to the legend of Electra who, along with her brother Orestes seeks to avenge her father Agamemnon's death at the hands of her mother, Clytemnestra, and of her mother's lover, Aegisthus. Giraudoux claimed that, before beginning his play, he had bought all of the main literary works that discussed the topic of Electra. However, he maintained that he did not have the time to read them and that he based his play on remembrances of the legend from material he had read during his schooldays.[15] Whether that is so or not, it is known that the playwright had a prodigious memory, and in its general outlines, Giraudoux's *Electra* does follow the story line of the well-known legend found in the Greek playwrights.[16] However, he did make some important changes. In the Greek versions, Electra is aware of the guilt of Clytemnestra and Aegisthus from the beginning. In Giraudoux's recounting, she is told that her father has had an accident — she suspects something more, and the development of the play deals with her search for the truth. In addition, Electra becomes a much stronger character in Giraudoux's play, rigidly and unswervingly pursuing total justice. Orestes, on the other hand, is weak willed and barely committed to her cause. And, while Aegisthus has little to do in the Greek tragedies, he assumes an important role in Giraudoux's work.

It was probably essential that Giraudoux make these changes so that he could construct his play along the lines with which he was most familiar. As in the rest of his dramatic works, *Electra* is a debate of a problem, a discussion of an issue in which each party hopes to convince the other of his position. In this drama of the absolute and the relative, total truth is placed in conflict with compromise. Again, as in his other writings, there is no clear-cut resolution of the problem.

Although Electra is twenty-one and presumably more mature than earlier Giraudoux heroines, she shares the single-mindedness of purpose associated with adolescence. Justice becomes her ideal, and she is unyielding and inflexible in its pursuit. In fact, she makes us think of Judith, with whom she shares many characteristics. Electra is a *femme à histoires,* a tenacious, difficult human being who causes ruin to anyone in her path. Although she represents truth and duty, she also typifies unhappiness, because she cannot be content with hypocrisy or lies. As one of the characters in the play states: "Upon seeing Electra, I feel all the crimes I've ever committed since the cradle moving around inside me" (*T* II, 20). At the beginning of the play, Electra does not yet understand what her role is to be but she is in the state where she is about to "declare herself." Symbolizing absolute justice, Electra places herself in opposition to relative justice, to those people who are willing to accept compromise, those who feel that accommodation is essential for daily living, even if such an action requires overlooking evil. Aegisthus takes up this side of the debate, and he maintains that society cannot tolerate a person like Electra. Real happiness, he comments, lies in not causing a disturbance, in not being noticed, in avoiding the awakening of the gods who watch over the country. As in *Tiger at the Gates,* the gods are generally indifferent to what is taking place, remaining in the background. However, Aegisthus notes, once they are disturbed, they unleash wars, plague, famine. In so doing, they always attack the wrong people, indicating that, besides being detached from humanity, they are also irresponsible. Electra's fault is that she will awaken these gods, and nothing but trouble will ensue.

In the first act, it is clear that the intransigent, demanding Electra can never accept the compromise that Aegisthus represents. Because the audience knows the legend, it is aware that Aegisthus, along with Clytemnestra, really did murder Agamemnon, and its sympathies remain entirely with Electra at this point. In the second act, Giraudoux suddenly changes the situation and the issue becomes much less clear. Electra has now found her role; she understands what happened to her father and she will pursue her justice with even more intensity. However, just as she has "declared herself," so has Aegisthus. Like Electra, he has found his essence. Argos is under attack by the Corinthians, and only Aegisthus can save the country. Since the people of Argos will not rally around a woman as their ruler, Aegisthus plans to marry Clytemnestra and to lead the country to victory. Having suddenly discovered his purpose in life, he is transformed: "Here is what I was given this morning — to me, a sensualist, a parasite, a cheat: I was given a country where I feel pure, strong, perfect, a homeland; and this homeland of which I was ready henceforth to be its servant, of which I am suddenly king, I swear to live, to die ... to save it" (*T* II, 75). At this moment, Aegisthus feels that he needs Electra's approval more than that of anyone else. Now that he is reaching his own form of purity, Electra is the only one to whom he feels close. If she will decide not to pursue her revenge, thus allowing him to rule Argos, it will mean that her country will be saved from attack. Aegisthus even offers to let her have her retribution on him following his defense of the country. Yet, Electra, the pure, cannot accept this sudden change, and she refuses to compromise.

There is another reason that she will not agree — Electra will not go along with Aegisthus because she has an almost insane hatred of her mother, Clytemnestra, and she is now on the point of bringing about Clytemnestra's downfall. Throughout the course of the play, Electra has been trying to discover the truth about her father's death. Clytemnestra knows the answer but, up to the very end, the mother lies, attempting to avoid any responsibility. Each scene between mother and daughter is one of increasing conflict, as the two women thrust and parry. As two human beings, they are very similar — in the final analysis Clytemnestra, like Electra, has spent her life alone. At first, Clytemnestra appeals to Electra as another woman, an approach that Electra brutally rejects, as she will everything that pertains to being female. Electra asks her mother over and over if she ever loved her father. Echoing a point raised in *Tiger at the Gates,* Giraudoux implies that everything may be worthwhile in this imperfect world if only two people love one another, if only there is a time of oneness. But, this is not the case of Clytemnestra and Agamemnon, and Electra finally understands the situation when she listens to an argument between two secondary characters, the Judge of the Tribunal and his unfaithful wife, Agatha. In admitting to her husband that she has a lover, Agatha explains why: "The sorrel eaten by my lover becomes ambrosia.... And everything which is soiled when my husband touches it comes out purified from his [my lover's] hands or from his lips... Myself included" (*T* II, 68). Electra now knows why Clytemnestra was never able to bear Agamemnon. She, too, found everything soiled when he touched it, he was impure in her eyes.

In the climactic scene between the two women, Clytemnestra admits that she hated Agamemnon, that she found him pompous, indecisive, and foolish. But her real reason is very typical of Giraudoux's turn of mind: "A woman belongs to everybody. There is precisely one man to whom she does not belong. The only man to whom I did not belong was the king of kings, the father of fathers, it was he! From the day he came to take me from my house, with his curly beard, with that hand with the little finger always raised, I hated him" (*T* II, 85). She continues to explain how these characteristics drove her to hatred — his little finger was always raised, even when he made love to her she could feel only four fingers on her back; and his beard, even when wet, never became smooth. As in *Tiger at the Gates,* Giraudoux playfully but seriously notes that major decisions are often made for trifling reasons. All the years of their marriage Clytemnestra has carried the lie of her love for him when there was nothing but hatred in her heart. Having arrived at her truth, Electra will have her revenge: Orestes will kill Clytemnestra and Aegisthus, and justice will be accomplished. At the same time, however, it now becomes clear that Electra's hatred of Clytemnestra and her need for justice were motivated by an almost erotic love for her father, resulting in a rejection of her mother and of matters feminine.[17] Giraudoux, perhaps unwittingly, picks up the idea of the Electra complex, making it a basis of the tragedy.

Which side in the conflict does the dramatist take? As in most of his works, the answer remains ambiguous, and the final passage in *Electra* underlines this ambiguity. In this last moment, Wife Narses asks Electra:

WIFE NARSES: What is it called, when day begins, like today, and everything is ruined, everything is destroyed, and yet the air can be breathed; and people have lost all, the city is burning, the innocents are killing each other, but nevertheless the guilty ones are dying, in a corner of the day which is rising?
ELECTRA: Ask the beggar. He knows.
THE BEGGAR: It has a very beautiful name, Wife Narses. It is called "dawn". (*T* II, 91–92)

One interpretation of the passage is that Electra was indeed right in her relentless pursuit of justice, her absolute truth, and that life has no meaning if it is not based on total purity. When the Beggar, a Giraudoux spokesman in the play, refers to dawn, he is alluding to the idea that, once evil has been removed, man will be able to start anew. Moreover, if we return to Giraudoux's political concerns when he wrote the play, it is possible to see that Electra possesses the high moral principles necessary to take her country out of its corruption and disgrace, the same type of principles needed in France at that period, according to Giraudoux, to take the country out of the morass into which it had fallen. Electra may be a thorn in everyone's side, but it is her role and she must fulfill it for the betterment of humanity.

A second and equally possible interpretation is that Giraudoux rejects Electra and her position. In spite of his marked turn toward pessimism, the writer could never have accepted a person of such extremes as Electra. In the final analysis, the conflict of the absolute and the relative is very much like the conflict of the ideal and the real, but presented in more practical terms. In his previous writings, the dramatist chose an idealized reality as man's final goal; here, he probably chooses the relative, the position of compromise. Aegisthus's point of view is probably that of Giraudoux: Electra's frightening egotism can never finally be that of her author's. In fact, throughout all of his work, Giraudoux seems to distinguish between those heroines like Alcmène and Isabelle who know how to love and those like Helen, Judith, and Electra, who do not.[18] Electra cares only for her father, but she cannot extend this to humanity at large. Moreover, her love for her father approaches an almost psychological condition and makes us think of Freudian theories, all the more reason for Giraudoux to reject her.

Although the critical reaction to the play was not totally favorable, *Electra* was a successful followup to *Tiger at the Gates,* and the drama ran for several months after its opening on May 13, 1937, at the Théâtre de l'Athénée in Paris. By now, the public had learned to accept the more tragic side of its once optimistic playwright.

V   The Realities of Love: Cantique des cantiques

On October 13, 1938, Giraudoux had the honor of seeing one of his plays presented at the famous Comédie-Française in Paris. For the occasion, the dramatist turned to his familiar structure: a young woman must make a choice between two men — the one representing an almost perfect ideal, the other a seemingly bland reality. As in all these tales, the woman chooses reality, although she does so reluctantly. However, while one part of the theme is by now too familiar, another part continues the playwright's recent and interesting preoccupation with the couple and with the difficulties of the male-female relationship.

For the title, *Cantique des cantiques (Song of Songs),* Giraudoux was obviously inspired by the biblical *Song of Solomon,* but other than that, the work has little in common with the Old Testament book. In this one act play, a dignified, wealthy, middle-aged gentleman (who resembles Giraudoux himself in many respects) is waiting in a chic Parisian café for the arrival of his mistress, Florence. A young man, Jerome, appears first and announces to the gentleman, called the president, that Florence has decided to leave the president and marry Jerome. After Jerome leaves to buy her flowers, Florence arrives and admits that what he said is true. She plans to go through with the wedding in spite of the fact that she admires the president much more. In fact, when she compares the two men, Jerome comes off a poor second. He is good-natured, but naive; he has no imagination; he shows no curiosity about Florence's past and is not at all suspicious of her. In brief, he is pedestrian, as Florence observes: "He never has any plans. He constantly studies the weather, minutely, by the thermometer, but he never goes out, never takes off, never vanishes" (*T* II, 181).

The president, on the other hand, is perfection itself in her eyes. He is serenity, strength, intelligence, discretion. Like the ghost in *Intermezzo,* the president has "something immortal, something invulnerable." But Jerome does have one quality lacking in the president — youth — and here it is likely that Giraudoux also must have been experiencing some of this same distress of middle age and empathized with the character of the president. Florence is confused because she knows that she does not love Jerome even though she will marry him. The president clarifies the situation for her: "That is not your love. Your love is quite different. It resembles us. It is an agreement, a consent, a feeling of ease. But it is love. You love Jerome with the love of another" (*T* II, 183). Florence's love for Jerome is that of the real world, a world that unfortunately cannot be ignored. Although it may not be the best expression of her love, it is her reality and she must accept it. Moreover, the young man, like the controller in *Intermezzo,* has his own attractions. He represents a chance of renewal, a sense of purity, for Florence will now be his wife rather than somebody's mistress (in this respect she makes us think of Nelly in *The Liar*). In addition, Jerome has a certain affinity with nature, always an enticement for the Giraudoux heroines.

To a great extent, *Song of Songs* is a repetition of many of the same elements we have seen before. However, the question of love and the difficulties of the male-female relationship are clearly topics that the writer cannot abandon in this last phase of his writing, probably because they have taken on such painfully personal meaning to him.

VI   *The Final Novel:* Choix des élues

The last novel that Giraudoux wrote was also his most somber. *Choix des élues (The Chosen Ones),* written in 1937–1938, reflects the writer's darker view of life. Once again, departure is the main theme, and this time it represents an almost unbearable need to escape everyday reality. Whereas Suzanne or Isabelle had their moment of the ideal as part of their adolescence, returning to a reality that they were generally willing to accept, Edmée, the mature protagonist of *The Chosen Ones,* returns to an infinitely more complicated and difficult existence.

Undoubtedly, Giraudoux's personal life had much to do with the tone of the novel. His marriage had disintegrated, and it is known that the author had his own method of flight, either through trips around the world as required by his diplomatic career or simply by leaving his family for weeks on end.[19] Moreover, later, in the last months of his life, he moved out of the family apartment entirely and into a hotel. Edmée's abandonment of family in the novel may possibly indicate many of Giraudoux's own wishes. A second theme in the work, but one almost as important, involves Claudie, Edmée's daughter, and the changes in her personality and in her relationship with her mother during Claudie's childhood and adolescence. Such a topic may have as its source Giraudoux's dealings with his own son, Jean-Pierre.[20]

The Chosen Ones begins at a birthday party for Edmée, the wife of Pierre, an engineer. They live with their children, Jacques and Claudie, in a pleasant city in California and, seemingly, are a happy family. On her thirty-third birthday, Edmée experiences a feeling of distress, a realization that matters are no longer bearable for her: "And suddenly this anguish, that she thought came from their [her family's] absence, now came back to her in their presence.... Grief overcame her.... Lord, please don't let it come from their presence!" (*OR* II, 641). Edmée soon begins to act erratically: she starts a harmless flirtation with Frank Warrin, a painter; she leaves her husband to spend a day in the park with her daughter, experiencing unusual joy in the separation. A brilliant man, Pierre is nonetheless unperceptive and has little understanding of his wife. Because of his training as an engineer, he is able to resolve complex technical problems easily, but he is rigid and uncomprehending on a human level, and Edmée's need to go beyond her ordinary life bewilders him. Although Pierre vaguely senses her unrest, he is unable to grasp sufficiently the seriousness of the situation. He urges her to take a trip with the Seeds, a wealthy couple who have asked Edmée to visit them. She takes Claudie with her and prepares to start a new life, not planning to return. Edmée realizes that she must leave in order to avoid what life has planned for her. She can imagine only too clearly the humdrum existence with her family and is therefore all the more determined to escape her fate.

Edmée heads for Hollywood, where she pursues a successful career as a technical adviser in a motion picture studio. For a while, her life is blissful, especially because she has her daughter, Claudie, with her, and at this point, the daughter adores the mother: "Both of them lived a life of great closeness, like that of a mother and daughter in nature. Edmée refused all luncheon invitations because she had an urgent lunch every day with her daughter. Claudie missed school because she had an invitation that she could not turn down every afternoon with her mother" (*OR* II, 721). In effect, they are Giraudoux's "chosen ones." They have found their earthly paradise away from husband, son, father, or brother.

But reality is too strong, and eventually it breaks this idyll. Edmée reexperiences the feeling of anguish, and surprisingly enough, she realizes that the pain is related to her daughter. Claudie had always been her support, her security. Now her daughter is growing up, and there must be a separation. Claudie has changed, as Edmée sadly observes: "I have near me a little god of indifference, of scorn, of forgetfulness" (*OR* II, 731). Edmée leaves Hollywood for San Francisco, where the transformation in Claudie grows worse. She is now like everyone else, as one of her teachers tells Edmée: "Your daughter no longer knows how to fly in the air! . . . Your daughter no longer feeds herself with the dew; she is no longer tall like the pine trees, she no longer shines like the sun. She can no longer be distinguished from any other girl" (*OR* II, 737-38). At this point, Edmée has a real affair with Frank Warrin, partly arranged by Claudie. However, whether out of jealousy or simply becaue of another personality change, Claudie becomes openly hostile to, and in revolt against, her mother. In an interesting reversal, the *jeune fille* of previous Giraudoux novels and plays no longer possesses the charms we have come to expect. The adolescence of one's life, formerly a period of great imagination, takes on a decidedly different perspective.

The story line takes a new direction: Edmée leaves her daughter (who no longer wants to remain with her mother in any event), and she eventually ends up as a housekeeper. In the interval, she has also seen her son again, now grown up, a university student, and engaged to be married. Jacques has come to ask that Edmée return to the family. Seeing him as an adult after the passage of several years, she immediately realizes that he is a younger version of her husband and that he shares the same lack of perception. Jacques has never understood why she left and has assumed that her departure was caused by a great love affair. Edmée now feels that Jacques was sent to her as a "sign" that her flight is over. She recalls a bizarre painting that she saw in her grandfather's salon. In the painting, a Russian countess follows her daughter-in-law to an inn where the daughter-in-law has run away with a music teacher. The countess has gone there to force the young woman to return home to the countess's son so that the family honor can be preserved. In the caption under the picture, the music teacher is identified as Abalstitiel. In Edmée's mind, Jacques becomes the countess, Edmée the daughter-in-law, and Abalstitiel the ideal that she has been seeking. Abalstitiel, a name with both Russian and biblical overtones,[21] symbolizes the unknown.

Like all the Giraudoux heroines, Edmée eventually returns to her real life with Pierre. However, unlike the other protagonists, she can find no happiness upon her return. It is only with a very sad heart that she reassumes her position in the family. She will be the Edmée of former times, but she can do so only by a supreme lie, leading the life of a Judith or Clytemnestra. She has returned, not but of love for Pierre, but only because her Abalstitiel, her ideal, has left her. Pierre has not changed; he does not understand the reason for her return and, as a result, is very careful not to disturb her. Jacques has married, and Claudie has also come back, wed to a student from Berkeley. In the final scene, Giraudoux ironically groups the cheerless family around another celebration: the baptism of Claudie's child. This becomes a new period of distress for Edmée as she recognizes that Claudie is beginning to experience some of the same signs that Edmée herself had shown earlier, and it is evident that Claudie will some day abandon her family, just as her mother did. Abalstitiel, the attraction of the unknown, is returning, and Edmée can only look upon her daughter with sorrow.

This final summation of Giraudoux's ideas in novelistic form is rich and complex. In spite of the fact that the writer had used the theme of departure so many times previously, he was still able to make it fresh and compelling, probably because it always represented such a deep part of his inner being. What had started as the reactions of a young man to the world around him had become the perceptive, troubled observations of a man in his middle years. Edmée and Claudie, the "chosen ones," superior to humanity, have nothing but sadness awaiting them. In spite of their attempts, they cannot escape reality. Giraudoux felt this same burden and expressed it in his writings. The charm — and harmony — found in *Amphitryon 38* or *Intermezzo* now tended to disappear. Although the author would continue to write works of sparkling wit and whimsy, the remaining publications would also be filled with greater irony and deeper pessimism.

VII   *The End of the Dream:* Ondine

The subject of Giraudoux's next play, *Ondine,* was suggested to him by Louis Jouvet and Madeleine Ozeray, an actress who had appeared in some of the dramatist's works. Mlle Ozeray had had a dream dealing with her childhood remembrances, and the dream recalled to Jouvet a tale written by the German writer, La Motte-Fouqué, on Ondine.[22] The director thought that, if this were turned into a play, it would provide an excellent part for Mlle Ozeray, and he urged Giraudoux to write it. It is likely that the topic did not interest the writer: he had already abandoned German Romanticism as a source of his theater, and he probably approached this retelling of the Ondine legend, so similar in theme to many of his previous works, with some reluctance.

However, once having done so, he made the work very much his own, for the subject had long fascinated him. The original source of the Ondine story comes from a medieval legend with which Giraudoux first came into contact when he was studying at the Sorbonne. At that time, he had read the *Undine* of La Motte-Fouqué.[23] In 1907[24] Charles Andler, the director of Giraudoux's German studies, asked the student to write a critical commentary on the topic. Although the paper was never completed, a rough draft of such an essay was found among Giraudoux's papers.[25] The idea of the Ondine or water sprite remained with the author in one form or another for a number of years. In *My Friend from Limousin,* he made several references to it. Two years later, Stephy, one of the principal characters in *Jerome Bardini,* seems to become like a water sprite for a time. An Ondine is also mentioned in the final version of *Intermezzo,* and more interestingly, an Ondine actually appears as a character in the early versions of the 1933 comedy.

Thus, although the subject of *Ondine* may have been imposed on him from outside, it was nevertheless a part of his personal interests, and he quickly adapted it to express his current mood. *Ondine* states quite clearly that the synthesis of the opposites, the union of the ideal and the real, long hoped for by the writer, is an impossible dream and the dramatist places the responsibility squarely on humanity's shoulders.

A look at the changes he made in the legend gives some indication of the playwright's intent. In the original German tale, some of the spirits found in nature lack souls, which they must have in order to be saved from destruction on the day of the Last Judgment. A female spirit may obtain a soul if she marries a human being. However, if the man she marries is discourteous to her near a body of water, she must return to the spirit world and, if he takes a human wife, the Ondine is obliged to kill him. La Motte-Fouqué infused the tale with his form of Romanticism, adding in particular a mystic or religious overtone. However, in the main, he followed the legend: the water sprite joins man through love, thereby possessing a soul, and remains eternally united with him, even in death.

Naturally, Giraudoux, in his versions, rejected any religious overtone, and he changed the reason for the Ondine's entrance into the human world: she does not need a soul, but she wants to be a part of humanity and is willing to forgo her purity as a spirit to obtain this goal. Unlike previous Giraudoux novels or plays, in which the human being tries to contact the realm of the unknown, in this case the world of the imagination tries to fit into reality. However, the Ondine finds that the human world is too limited, too narrow to accept her. The human environment, Giraudoux concludes somberly, does not contain enough dimension to absorb the world of the spirits; everyday reality is too restricted. It is as if the writer's final effort to merge the two sides has now definitively failed. Even when the universe tries to reach humanity, the attempt is futile. Giraudoux seems to be saying that the possibility of achieving some sort of victory over the degradation of reality has ended. And, for the first time, he closely links his recent theme of the problem of the couple with his lifelong dream of the union of the real and the ideal. In its own way, the inability of man and woman to develop a harmonious relationship also symbolizes the end of his dream.

It appears that the first act of the play came very easily to the dramatist, and he finished it by June of 1938.[26] Ondine is an adopted daughter of August and Eugenia, a simple couple who make their living by fishing. Although they love Ondine, they are constantly bewildered and amazed by her magical powers and her almost mystical association with the waters surrounding their cottage, not realizing that she comes from the world of the spirits. One rainy evening, Hans von Wittenstein, a knight errant, happens upon the home of August and Eugenia, asking for food and lodging. Hans is engaged to the king's adopted daughter, Bertha, but, as a prior condition to the marriage, he has to pass through a forest filled with danger to prove that he is truly worthy. Hans is a somewhat limited man with little sensitivity to nature. However, when Ondine arrives, she immediately declares her love for him and for humanity by crying out: "How handsome you are!," using the expression that is the basis of Giraudoux's later play, *The Apollo of Bellac*. The other Ondines try to persuade her to forsake Hans, for they know that she intends to marry him and enter the human world. If Hans should ever deceive her, which seems inevitable, he will have to die. Ondine understands this, but she is determined to enter this new world because she has complete confidence in Hans. For his part, Hans is attracted to Ondine and to nature to an extent that he has never known before.

Giraudoux apparently had difficulty with the second act, in which he planned to show what happens to Ondine when she returns to Hans's world. However, he resolved this problem by using the play within a play technique. After his honeymoon with Ondine, Hans has decided to present his fifteen year old bride to the court of the king, where a celebration and entertainment have been planned. Among the participants in the extravagant event is an illusionist who is the king of the Ondines in disguise. The illusionist has the power to take moments from the future life of Hans and Ondine and to present them at this time for the diversion of the court. In that sense, he plays the role of fate or destiny, controlling the passage of time, demonstrating what will happen to man. In the illusionist's presentation of the future, Hans sees Bertha again, becoming attached to her and to her world once more, and Ondine's happiness is destroyed. In sharp contrast to the imaginative ambience of the first act, the future reality created by the illusionist offers nothing but cruel deception: the passage of time brings about the end of the mythical love of Hans and Ondine, and Hans's eventual return to Bertha symbolizes his abandonment of the supernatural and the life of the unknown.[27] More than anything else, the play within a play indicates the impossibility of the union of the real and the ideal. In addition, the court, the world in which Hans normally functions, is a bitter disillusionment. Its chaos and confusion only accentuate the deceit and hypocrisy that are its basis. It is not surprising that Ondine should find that she cannot fit into this milieu. Her naturalness, an expression of truth, is odious to the hypocritical realm of the court. She particularly comes into conflict with Bertha in front of her supposed father, the king. The illusionist comes to her rescue when he reveals that the Princess Bertha is actually the long lost daughter of August and Eugenia, and consequently, Bertha must now leave the court. Ondine, seeing that her husband is still attracted to his former fiancée, decides that the only way to keep his love is to do just the opposite of what would normally be done: she invites Bertha to accompany Hans and herself when they leave the palace.

Giraudoux still had to complete a third act for the play. Jean-Pierre states that his father finished the first two acts without enthusiasm and that he half seriously asked his son to give him an idea for the third.[28] The playwright's inspiration finally came from the trial scene of Heinrich von Kleist's play, *Kätchen von Heilbronn*.[29] By now, Ondine has left Hans, for she understands that he will marry Bertha. She leaves without a trace but invents a story, telling him before her departure that she has deceived him with another man. When she is eventually captured by a fisherman in his net, she is brought to trial on charges of witchcraft. Ondine tries vainly to save Hans from the fate that awaits him at the hands of the king of the Ondines by saying again that she, not Hans, was the first to betray. However, her lies are evident, and according to what was predicted, Hans must die. But Hans willingly accepts his death — he has lost his interest in living. The greatness that he had had in his contact with the nonhuman world has been lost — he now clearly sees the sordidness of reality. At the same moment, Ondine loses her contact with the human world and returns to the domain of the water spirits. Just before her break with humanity, she sees

Hans lying on the ground, dead. By now, she has forgotten their relationship and says: "How pleasing he is to me!... Can't we give him back his life?" On being told no, she answers: "That's too bad! How I would have loved him!" (*T* II, 282).

When *Ondine* was first performed, at the Théâtre de l'Athénée in Paris on April 27, 1939, it was immediately recognized as one of Giraudoux's more beautiful and poetic plays and had a successful run. *Ondine* is also important when we consider the progression of Giraudoux's dramatic writings, for it marks the end of his hopes. Although Giraudoux utilized once again his basic theme and once more took German Romanticism as his source, the message is unmistakable: man has lost his battle for the ideal; reality will triumph. Life cannot contain the domain of the imagination because mortals are too narrow, too limited in outlook. And, foreshadowing *Sodom and Gomorrah*, Giraudoux suggests that the failure of the couple to maintain a harmonious union must also share a great deal of the responsibility for the end of the dream. Wolfgang Sohlich analyzes the role of man and woman in Giraudoux's world: "Man, in order to find his path to human happiness, must constantly transcend himself to find himself and he must do this as a unit, as man and woman, as man who does and who dreams, as one who lives a human reality transformed by the presence of the ideal."[30] The desire to merge man and woman is the wish to join the real and the ideal. As in most of Giraudoux's writings, the male represents the rational, common sense, everyday life, and the female becomes the unknown, the transcendence, the unconscious. If a human being can be composed of transcendence (the unknown, the female) and immanence (reality, the male), he has the possibility to go beyond the degradation of reality.[31] The two together provide the opportunity for a better existence. Hans's and Ondine's separation suggests that the possibility is lost, probably forever.

The future looked bleak for the writer, both on the personal side and on the international scene. *Ondine,* with its German source, must have reminded the dramatist of his once shining hopes for French-German unity. Although it is difficult to date when the dramatist wrote the play in relation to the international crisis of 1938, it is known that Hitler signed the Munich agreement on September 29 of that year, before Giraudoux had finished his third act.[32] *Ondine* could never have had a "happy" ending.

VIII   *The Ultimate Problem — The Couple:* Sodome et Gomorrhe

What Giraudoux started to say in *Ondine,* he finished in *Sodome et Gomorrhe (Sodom and Gomorrah,* 1943). In *Ondine,* he noted the break between man and the universe and suggested that the blame for this separation be placed upon man and woman. In *Sodom and Gomorrah,* he leaves no doubt that the couple is the source of the problem, and this play is thus a work of utter despair. In many respects, Giraudoux's world had collapsed around him, and at this particular moment, he could no longer brush it over with his usual veneer of wit and humor. Although the play had its premiere on October 11, 1943, at the Théâtre Hébertot in Paris, the dramatist actually began it considerably earlier. He apparently developed the outline of the drama immediately following the writing of *Ondine,* during the rehearsals of that play in 1939.[33] The dramatist then dropped it, no longer able to write because of the impending war. However, he picked the work up again and finished it in the winter of 1940–1941.[34] Because of the timing of the first performance, many critics mistakenly saw *Sodom and Gomorrah* as a commentary on the occupation of France. But, the play is, instead, one of the deepest expressions of the writer's personal anguish.

The drama exists on one level as a reflection of the problems that Giraudoux saw in his own relationship with his wife. Madame Giraudoux herself noted in an interview that her husband experienced a sense of shame in speaking to her about it.[35] On another level, this separation between man and woman underlines the disharmony between mankind and the universe. In *Sodom and Gomorrah,* the couple becomes the main cause of man's break with the cosmos, the reason for his lack of inner peace. The problem, Giraudoux argues, is that the original, primitive union of the couple has been lost. As one of his characters states: "There never were separate creatures. There never was anything other than the couple. God did not create man and woman one after the other, nor one from the other. He created two twin beings united by strips of flesh which He separated later, in a moment of confidence, the day He created tenderness" (*T* II, 329). If it were possible to return to this former state, at least in the sense that a man and woman could develop a perfect union, some of the harmony of the universe could be reestablished.

It is likely that Giraudoux found this theory in Plato's *Sympo-*

sium, where the idea is put forth that God first created an andro-
gyne and then separated it. It is also probable that the dramatist found another important source in Léon Ebreo.[36] Ebreo
(1460–1521), the son of Isaac Abravanel, a Jewish theologian and
biblical commentator, was famous as the author of *Dialogues on
Love,* which contain the idea that only through love can man reach
a union with God, an idea also found in Plato. Ebreo's point is that
man was originally created one, both male and female at the same
time and that, at a certain moment, there was an essential basic
unity and oneness in the human being. Obviously, Giraudoux did
not consider the couple important as a means of reaching God, but
rather as a way of rediscovering a lost state of innocence or harmony, of recapturing the sense of perfection of the universe, of
transcending the degradation of reality. To express this theme, the
playwright turned, interestingly enough, to the Bible and to the
passage on Sodom and Gomorrah from Genesis, Chapters 18–19.
In this section, God destroys the two cities by fire because of their
carnal wickedness, specifically because of homosexuality. However, the dramatist simply took this passage as a point of departure
in order to explore his particular preoccupations, and he dropped
the homosexual reference entirely.

In the prelude to *Sodom and Gomorrah,* an archangel explains
that God is angry because He created a world of couples and He
now finds man and woman divided. However, the archangel continues, if God can find a truly happy marriage, He will spare the
two cities; otherwise, He will cause destruction and ruin. Two
couples in particular attract His attention: Lia and Jean, Ruth and
Jacques. At this point, Lia no longer loves Jean, and in fact, her
love has turned to hatred. He is different from what he was when
they were married, and she feels that she no longer knows him — he
is not the ideal she had hoped to find. At the same time, Ruth finds
her husband dull and unchanging. The two couples decide to
exchange partners to see if that will help, but, like everything else
between man and woman, it fails.

Lia, the central character, turns to the angel for her happiness,
hoping to find peace with the unknown. However, the angel turns
her away, warning her of the seriousness of the situation. Unlike
Isabelle, who could find a real measure of satisfaction in her humble life with the controller, Lia is unable to tolerate her reality with
Jean. Moreover, like most of the dramatist's female protagonists,
she is stronger than the male, more forceful in personality, more

gifted in debate; Jean is more passive, less sure of himself. Lia notes one of her main complaints about men: "Oh God, if you never want a woman to raise her voice, then create finally an adult man! What do you want us to do with this maniacal son whom we have neither born nor nourished!" (*T* II, 327). However, Lia's strength ultimately forces us to withdraw from her: we find her unpleasant and disagreeable.

As in many Giraudoux plays, there is a *sosie,* a double found among the secondary characters who expresses the same ideas found in the protagonists. In *Sodom and Gomorrah,* in an interlude in the second act, Giraudoux introduces the character of Delilah, who tells us why she and Samson make the "perfect" couple. Her reasons parallel Lia's: Delilah observes ironically that the strong and powerful Samson is like all men, he needs a master. She has taken on this task and treats him like a child, making all other women seem odious to him. As in Lia's case, Delilah is distasteful to us, and Giraudoux seems to suggest that the woman must bear the ultimate responsibility for the separation of the couple.

The angels are still seeking one perfect marriage to represent humanity, and they continue to turn to Lia and Jean. In a half-hearted attempt, the two try to become what God wants, but their attempt fails. Their love is over — there are too many lies, too many deceits between them. There is to be no salvation for humanity, and all the men and women separate on one side of the room or the other according to sex, to be killed when God sends his wrath down upon them. In a final ironic touch, after everyone has died, we can still hear the voice of Jean saying, "Pardon me, skies! What a night!" and Lia's response, "Thank you, heavens! What a dawn!" (*T* II, 340). Even at the final moment, man and women are on opposite sides. The end of the world in *Sodom and Gomorrah* is a moment of revelation, as Jean notes: "They call the end of the world the day when the world shows itself for what it is: explosive, fragile, combustible, just as they call war the day when the human soul gives itself over to its true nature" (*T* II, 316). This end of the world also reveals in startling fashion the extent of Giraudoux's gloom. He wrote two more plays containing his typical wit and sparkle, especially the extremely successful *The Madwoman of Chaillot.* But he could not remove himself from reality, and with increasing frequency, his mood was pessimistic.

When *Sodom and Gomorrah* was performed in 1943, Louis Jouvet was on a tour in South America, and the dramatist had to do without the vital services of his director. However, in spite of a lukewarm press, the play managed to find a public, and it was still being performed on January 31, 1944, when Giraudoux died, thus becoming the last drama to be presented during his lifetime. Unfortunately, the work does not have much appeal today, seeming too somber and heavy in tone. With the Giraudoux banter and wit gone, the play is less effective. The author was at his best when his diverse and imaginative style could reflect his sense of the infinite possibilities of the universe, the freedom of the unknown. As he became too preoccupied with his problems in reality, his writing also lost some of its strength.

IX *The Willful Optimism:* L'Apollon de Bellac

Between the composition of *Sodom and Gomorrah* in 1939 and its first performance in 1943, Giraudoux wrote a charming one act play called *L'Apollon de Bellac (The Apollo of Bellac,* 1946). The stubbornly optimistic short piece contrasts sharply — and pleasantly — with the somber and bleak tone of the other work, indicating that the dramatist was determined to find a more cheerful reality amidst the gloom surrounding him.

In February 1942, Giraudoux placed a telephone call to Louis Jouvet, who had left Paris during the occupation of France and was on tour in Rio de Janeiro. Giraudoux informed his director that he was sending him the manuscript of a play that he hoped could be presented. At the time, the title was incomplete, simply called *L'Apollon de. . .,* Giraudoux telling Jouvet that he, Jouvet, could find the appropriate name himself. On June 16, 1942, the play received its first performance by Jouvet's company in Rio. At that time, it was entitled *The Apollo of Marsac,* in deference to Giraudoux's Limousin region. Later, in 1946, when it came time to publish the comedy, a copy of proofs that Giraudoux had worked on before his death was discovered. In these proofs, Giraudoux had listed the title as *L'Apollon de Bellac,* a reference to his birthplace.[37] After the war, the play received its first performance in Paris on April 19, 1947, Théâtre de l'Athénée.[38]

The Apollo of Bellac recalls the fantasy and delight of *Intermezzo.* The story line is purposely simple. Agnes, the heroine, is seeking office work and has come to the "Office of the Great and Small Inventors" to apply for a position. However, she has no special qualifications for secretarial work, and in addition, she possesses an inordinate fear of men. At the office, she meets the gentleman from Bellac, a strange, mysterious character similar to the ghost in *Intermezzo*. He advises Agnes on ways to obtain the secretarial position and on methods of controlling men. All she has to do is say: "How handsome you are." To her reply that people will not believe her, the gentleman from Bellac responds: "They will all believe it. Everyone believes it in advance. Each man, even the ugliest, nourishes in himself a secret attachment directly with beauty. He will simply hear the word uttered aloud that his self-satisfaction has been saying secretly" (*T* II, 424). Fortified with this advice, Agnes starts practicing on objects like a chandelier or a telephone. Then, proceeding to human beings like the usher at the office and the general secretary of the firm, she finds that she has indeed discovered a successful technique. Finally, she takes on the president of the firm himself. The results are spectacular: he fires his disagreeable private secretary to give the position to Agnes, and he then breaks his engagement to his fiancée so that he can make Agnes his wife. However, she is not satisfied. She does not really care for the president, but turns instead toward the ideal, the gentleman from Bellac, just as Isabelle had also turned toward the ghost. However, this ideal is not to be, at least not for the moment. Agnes realizes that the gentleman from Bellac is "too brilliant and too grand" for her. And he disappears, so that she may resume the successful life that he has taught her. She will also be able, as the gentleman from Bellac notes, to find another "mediocre human being" like herself.

If nothing else, this quite typical Giraudoux play indicates that the whimsical, inventive, and subtle imagination of the dramatist was still present. Amidst the darkness of the early 1940s, *The Apollo of Bellac* and, later, *The Madwoman of Chaillot,* were indications that the dramatist's hopes could never be extinguished and that they would resurface sporadically.

X   *The Political Play:* La Folle de Chaillot

When he was writing *La Folle de Chaillot* (*The Madwoman of Chaillot,* 1945), Giraudoux was focusing his attention more and more on the problems of everyday living. Concerned for some time about urban difficulties, he undertook a series of articles on the situation of France, analyzing what could be done to improve the quality of life for its citizens (these articles will be discussed in a later section). In a France occupied by the Germans, the writer obstinately looked to the future and to ways in which man could hope in the midst of despair. At the same time, he felt the need to warn his fellow countrymen about the dangers they might be facing in the years following the war.

The Madwoman of Chaillot was one of the results of his thinking during the years shortly before his death. On the surface, this whimsical tale could appear rather slight and frivolous in its naive solutions to complicated problems. And indeed, some critics have seen the comedy as one of the less substantial of Giraudoux's full length plays.[39] However, like so much of his work, *The Madwoman of Chaillot* had a special, deeper meaning to the dramatist, which he chose to express in his usual amusing fashion. Moreover, the play contained enough solidity to touch a nerve in the public. When it was first presented in Paris on December 19, 1945, at the Théâtre de l'Athénée, its subject coincided perfectly with the time. France had just gone through one of the most tragic periods in its history. Besides the enormous loss of life during World War II, some of the French citizens had acted dishonorably during the German occupation of their country. Their collaboration with the Nazis was often accompanied by illegal financial activities and shameful and fraudulent business practices. Now that the war was over, the French emotions were understandably high over the exploitation of some of their countrymen, and they demanded justice. As a result, the question of right and wrong was viewed in somewhat basic terms in the interest of ridding the country of the corruption that had existed. Giraudoux's newest play, with its straightforward approach to good and evil and its facile solutions to problems, found its audience in the French public of that time. The occasion of the first performance was a major event. Louis Jouvet was back in Paris once again, after his exile during the war years, and he was once more going to direct a Giraudoux play, the first since the dramatist's death. An actress of considerable esteem, Marguérite Moréno, played the leading role to the greatest acclaim of her career, and the play ran for 297 performances, longer than any other Giraudoux work.

The writer chose to convey his warnings about France's future via a fairy tale, for, basically, *The Madwoman of Chaillot* is a fantasy about the triumph of the forces of good over the forces of evil. In the play, the Madwoman (the character was inspired by a bizarre lady whom the dramatist had seen one day on the streets of Paris

and whom he had never been able to find again) becomes the leader
of the "nice" people who must triumph over the "wicked" who are
out to destroy their way of life. These "nice" citizens include a rag-
picker, a washer of dishes, a sewerman, a flower girl — all the
small, humble people of Giraudoux's world who contribute the real
essence of life. In their fanciful approach to living, they represent
the poetry to be found in existence and are similar to the controller
in *Intermezzo*. Towering over all of the figures is the Countess
Aurelia, the Madwoman of Chaillot, dressed in her exaggerated
outfits — eccentric, preposterous, but possessing an understanding
of the real values of living.

Opposing them are the "evil" ones — the barons, the presidents,
the financiers — all representatives of the capitalist system, a surprisingly direct reference to reality on Giraudoux's part. This group
is now meeting at the Café Chez Francis in order to form a cartel to
obtain the oil that they are told rests directly underneath the café.
In order to secure this oil, they will have to destroy the beauty and
charm of the neighborhood. But nothing will stop them in their
quest to gain such an enormous financial prize. At first, the Madwoman is slow to recognize the problem and to respond to it, perhaps, as Agnès Raymond suggests, a reference to Giraudoux's own
timidity in speaking out during the war.[40] However, when Aurelia is
told of the intentions of the profiteers, she soon develops a scheme
of her own to preserve the way of life that the common people have
known. She summons several of her friends to a meeting in her
apartment in the Chaillot section of Paris. These friends, also identified as "madwomen," discuss the crisis with their own special
brand of nonsensical sense. In Aurelia's apartment, there is a trap
door that leads to the sewers of the city and from which people
cannot return. A mock trial is held in which the humble people of
the neighborhood enact the roles of the capitalist profiteers, who
are soon found guilty. Aurelia then invites all of these financial
barons to come to her apartment, telling them that they can exam-
ine the land beneath it for oil. They arrive, and she sends them
down to the "oil" through the trap door, which she promptly
closes on them. Through this symbolic means, the world has been
rid of profiteering and has been made pure once again.

On one level, *The Madwoman of Chaillot* is a delightful play:
man has recognized the enemy and has conquered. Following *The
Apollo of Bellac*, it is a special pleasure to find the author continuing in the inventive and fanciful style that marked his earlier writ-

ings and that would always remain his most distinctive characteristic. In fact, along with *Intermezzo, The Madwoman of Chaillot* illustrates the writer's sense of fantasy better than any other major play, for its fairy tale atmosphere allows the imagination to soar. The dramatist uses the unexpected and enjoyable twists and turns of his mind to full advantage. When the Countess Aurelia appears for the first time, dressed in her outlandish garb, and asks: "Are my bones ready, Irma?" (*T* II, 357), the spectator knows that he is off on a whimsical trip. Aurelia's defense of the joys of life is quintessential Giraudoux:

All living beings are lucky.... Of course, upon awakening, it is not always gay. While choosing your hair for the day in the Hindu jewel box, or while taking your teeth out of the only cup which you have left from the service setting after the move from Bienfaisance street, you may obviously feel a little out of place in this world.... But so that you may feel that life has called upon you, all you have to do is find in your mail a letter with the progress of the day. You write it yourself the night before, that's more reasonable." (*T* II, 367)

And the delightful nonsequiturs of the "madwomen" when they attempt to discuss a serious subject are a reflection of Giraudoux at his most sparkling.

The play appears to have been such a lark for the dramatist that it seems a startling turnabout from the other writings of that period. Following shortly after *Sodom and Gomorrah* and preceding *Duel of Angels,* the work is somewhat surprising in the sense that the dramatist appeared to change styles so suddenly. But, while *The Madwoman of Chaillot* turns to another, happier time, it is still very much a part of the last phase of his writing and deals with reality — this time, political reality. The dramatist has a message for his audience: be careful about the quality of your life, people are at work trying to take it away from you. In this work, his urban preoccupations are coupled with an attack on modern capitalism and the technological society in which people have lost their importance. In fact, the rather unexpected political militancy of the play has led some critics to undertake detailed analyses of its implications[41] and has even caused Jacques Body to see the comedy as a revolution in Giraudoux's writing that his death interrupted.[42]

It could be argued, however, that, paradoxically enough, at the very moment that the dramatist was being the most militant and supposedly dealing with reality, he was not discussing the most immediate and most important reality. The writer's concerns for urbanism and his worries about the capitalist control of one's life were problems for the future, after the war. Yet the presence of German forces on French soil at that period was an even greater worry for the general public. Understandably, the people of France were demoralized and defeated, and it seems as if the dramatist made a willful decision to transcend the sordidness of this too-present reality. It is as if, to the very end, the author was determined to avoid a direct confrontation with reality and, to the extent possible, to create his own reality. Even after having made the decision to treat life more directly, it still had to be on his own very special terms.

XI *The Final Play:* Pour Lucrèce

Giraudoux's last play, *Pour Lucrèce* (*Duel of Angels,* 1953),[43] is a return to his somber, hopeless mood. This final literary statement is a continuation of the despair of *Sodom and Gomorrah,* and the sparkle of *The Madwoman of Chaillot* has totally disappeared. Since the work was written in 1943, shortly before his death, at the height of World War II and while the author was living apart from his wife, the world seemed very desolate, and Giraudoux's response reflected the extent of his discouragement. It is also a possibility that the death of his mother on November 2, 1943, added to his sense of total distress. The dramatist's emotional attachment to her was strong and her passing must have cast a shadow over everything that he undertook.

He probably began composing the play while Edwige Feuillère, a leading actress of the French stage, was performing in *Sodom and Gomorrah.*[44] He wrote a part for Madame Feuillère as well as one for Madeleine Ozeray. Following Giraudoux's death on January 31, 1944, Jouvet requested permission to present the work, but Madame Giraudoux did not wish to release it. The approval for production was not given until 1953, by which time Jouvet had died and Jean-Louis Barrault had taken over as director. Edwige Feuillère eventually did appear in the play, along with Madeleine Renaud, on November 4, 1953, at the Théâtre Marigny in Paris. Barrault had an exceedingly difficult task in preparing *Duel of Angels.* Giraudoux had left three manuscripts of the work, all in an unfinished state because of his death. In addition, each version differed considerably from the other, and Barrault did not have the dramatist around to help him choose the correct reading. He finally selected the text that Jouvet had hoped to present, and he allowed the rehearsals to help shape the final form.[45] While there had been rumors that Giraudoux had only written an outline of the play and that the final version may have been someone else's handiwork, the existence of the three manuscripts disproved those reports.[46]

The play is certainly consistent with the rest of the dramatist's writing. The main theme, the necessity of purity and innocence in life, has been treated before, although never so bleakly. Lucile, the central character, is a sister to Electra and Judith, and her problems, although presented much more starkly, are not that far removed from those of Alcmene. Continuing the pattern found in this last phase of Giraudoux's writing, it is not destiny that destroys mankind, but man himself; his inhumanity to his fellow human beings has created the terrible problems of existence. What is relatively different this time is the solution to the situation: death. It is as if the dramatist has finally found the only certain way of transcending reality and finding purity — through this total and lasting escape.

Giraudoux found the inspiration for *Duel of Angels* in Roman legend in the story by Livy about Lucretia, a woman famous for her virtue. She is the victim of a rape by Sextus, son of the king, Lucius Tarquinius Superbus. Lucretia tells her husband and his friends of her shame and urges them to avenge her honor. Because of what has happened, she is no longer able to continue living and mortally stabs herself. The ensuing revolt drives the Tarquins from Rome, bringing about the downfall of royalty and the eventual establishment of the Roman Republic.

Giraudoux's Lucretia is named Lucile Blanchard, the wife of Lionel Blanchard, a public attorney living in Aix-en-Provence during the Second Empire. Lucile and her husband, both critical, unyielding people, are obsessed with the need to prevent licentiousness in the town. Dressed in white, she becomes the symbol of the total purity that she is seeking. Like Electra, she is a *femme à histoires,* refusing to compromise, denouncing impurity, pursuing her goals with unswerving directness. She possesses a strange, almost "divine" power of being able to detect immediately if anyone in her presence is impure, and if that is the case, Lucile denounces the person without delay. The effects of this "divine" power are strictly human, however, and her special gifts make life impossible for the inhabitants of this rather lazy town in the south of France.

In sharp contrast, Giraudoux has created the character of Paola, a sensuous, vital, beautiful woman who lives a life of wantonness and licentiousness. Paola's wickedness, in opposition to Lucile's purity, provides the needed conflict out of which the playwright creates the substance of his drama. Paola has been unfaithful to her husband, Armand, for some time. When she meets Lucile, the latter cannot contain her disgust, and she reveals Paola's infidelity to Armand. In order to have her revenge, Paola enlists the services of Count Marcellus, one of her former lovers and a notorious womanizer in Aix. She prepares a scheme in which she drugs Lucile and has her taken to the house of Barbetta, the procuress. When Lucile awakens, she is told that she was raped by Marcellus during her sleep, an incident that, in fact, did not take place. Understandably, Lucile, the epitome of purity and innocence, is in despair and insists that Armand avenge her. He challenges Marcellus to a duel and kills him. In the meantime, Lucile has confessed to her husband, who reacts angrily and is totally insensitive to the depths of her shame. Lucile now sees only one answer to the sordidness and wretchedness of life: she poisons herself. Before she dies, however, Paola reveals that the incident was invented and that Lucile was never raped. What makes the matter even more ironic is that Lucile, who was able to spot impurity in everyone else, was unable to tell that she herself was still pure, an overwhelming imperfection in her eyes. If nothing else, she is willing to accept her death because it is a way of arriving at the purity that she has lost. She also refuses to allow her husband to be told the truth, because he has shown himself to be so undeserving. In one way, though, Lucile actually has been violated, as the procuress Barbetta indicates: "You were indeed raped. Not by Marcellus.... But by the stupidity of men, the crudeness of men, the wickedness of men" (*T* II, 522).

Man and his treachery have made the world uninhabitable for those seeking purity. In addition, once again Giraudoux links the impurity in the world with the failure of the male-female relationship, this time raising the question of the fidelity of women. Faced with his own dreams collapsing around him, the writer, in his literature at least, sees death as the only means of retaining the perfection that reality takes away, a most pessimistic resolution of the problem and one that he had used only rarely in the past in his works.

Yet, this play, like most of Giraudoux's writings, contains its ambiguities. Lucile has certainly been betrayed by humanity, but

her intransigence and her inflexible attitude leave us somewhat unsympathetic; she has made life impossible for others, and it is difficult for us to react favorably to her position. In fact, it is hard to
feel much compassion for any of the characters in *Duel of Angels,*
most of whom are generally lifeless. What qualities they do possess
tend to seem disagreeable and unpleasant. Obviously, the dramatist
would have revised the play had his death not prevented it. Even so,
it is unlikely that he would have changed it to any great extent. The
work is meant to be a bitter attack on humanity, and in a sense, it
reflects a withdrawal from life. It is unfortunate that Giraudoux's
final literary message should be so despairing, but it is perhaps not
all that atypical of the writer who, in his inner being, could never
adjust to reality.

XII   *Giraudoux's Political and Social Reality*

During the last ten years of his life, as his plays and novels reflected a more direct reality, particularly one with man as its center,
Giraudoux also wrote a number of articles and gave a series of lectures dealing with life in the modern urban world.

In 1934, he delivered three lectures at the Université des
Annales[47] on the subject of women, entitled *La Française et la
France (The French Woman and France).*[48] In these talks, Giraudoux dealt with a topic of great concern to him: France's ability to
improve the quality of the lives of its people. Much of this improvement, he observes, can come from the French woman, who has the
knowledge and the practicality of this century. The roles of men
and women are changing. Formerly, women believed that men were
like gods; now they realize that men are often involved in humiliat-
ing and demeaning work. At one time, men thought that women
were weak; now they know that women are as intelligent and as
shrewd as they are. Giraudoux also sees women as being better able
to cope with the problems of the modern world. Because they have
had limited contact with the great problems faced by nations, they
are able to bring a fresh viewpoint and to find solutions that have
escaped the men. Reflecting his own heroines in novels and plays,
Giraudoux notes that women have the imagination to go beyond
the usual, the routine. They are capable of finding new paths, and
in fact, their extravagance is one of their important qualities.
Often, it is *les grandes folles* who can accomplish wonderful
improvements, an early reference to the protagonist in *The Mad-*

woman of Chaillot. France, Giraudoux concludes, needs its women to help the country, and men must avoid placing them in inferior roles.

In part, Giraudoux's ideas in *The Frenchwoman and France* are modern and can be related to today's world. But there is also a certain whimsical and simplistic approach that tends to lessen the impact of his points. Such is not the case, however, in his next major piece of writing dealing with political and social problems. In 1939, Giraudoux gave another series of lectures at the Université des Annales on the situation of France as he saw it at that moment, when it was passing through a difficult period. In these lectures, published under the title *Pleins Pouvoirs (Full Powers),* the author maintains that France has deteriorated badly, and he emphasizes the seriousness of its situation. It is interesting to note, though, that many of the problems that he discusses had been concerns of Giraudoux's for some time and that much of the material for these lectures came from articles that he had published in newspapers and journals as early as 1933.[49] For the lectures, he simply updated the material.

In essence, Giraudoux is dealing with the problem of keeping France a major power on the international scene. In order to do this, it is his opinion that people must not look outward to world problems but must rather consider the internal difficulties in which France finds herself. If the country can resolve its internal problems, it can then reestablish itself as an important nation. To deal with these difficulties, France must use its imagination, the writer once again reaffirming the value of the inventive mind. One of the first problems facing the nation is that of the declining population: the number of Frenchmen is not keeping pace with the increase in the number of inhabitants in the world. Because of the low birth rate and an inadequate health system, the country is not retaining its population.

A reason for this situation, Giraudoux insists, is that politicians are not thinking enough about the individual Frenchman and his problems. In fact, continues the writer, the politicians have no appreciation of the real issues facing man, particularly urban man. Since more and more people are living in cities, especially Paris, more thought must be given to city life. At this moment, Giraudoux states, France is not being maintained properly — it is not creating any beautiful new buildings, and it is tearing down the fine old ones. The achievements of the past are in danger because political leaders are too easily swayed by their electorate and, usually, only by a minority of the electorate at that. Moreover, not enough imagination is being used in creating work projects in order to build up the city. If the government can build projects that give man confidence in himself, then it will have achieved something of great value. These projects must also give an indication of the moral authority of France, so that the country appears energetic in the eyes of others.

In a strong statement, Giraudoux observes that one of the country's major problems is that France has lost its sense of morality, particularly its civic morality. For the world at large, the name "France" still invokes the idea of justice and honor. However, the word "Frenchman" calls forth a sense of disharmony, disunion, and corruption. The moral fiber of the country is under attack. In Paris, for example, the open spaces, so essential to the well-being of the city, are being covered with apartment buildings. The builders have obtained the support of some politicians, and a few people have succeeded in taking away the rights of five million Parisians. In Giraudoux's view, it is these few corrupt people who are ruining the life of the country and who are actually conspiring against the state. Their only interests are financial gain, and they share a disdain for the orinary Frenchman. France must now live for itself, and the French must realize that their country is a precious gift to be protected.

Full Powers displays a more practical side of the author of *Suzanne and the Pacific* and *Intermezzo*. His urban concerns, which actually dated as far back as 1918, accurately predicted the difficulties that France would face in the future. And Giraudoux correctly perceived the weakness in the moral fiber of his country and his countrymen. The work does, however, contain some oversimplifications and some startling statements that reflect the writer's conservative nature as well as his considerable innocence in international politics. In a curiously elitist, almost racist comment, Giraudoux maintains that France must try to "drive out any element which could corrupt a race that owes its values to selection and improvements over twenty centuries."[50] France, he continues, is swarming with people who add nothing to its life. Nevertheless, he is willing to admit immigrants who have something to offer, such as writers or painters. In another statement that reflects his naiveté and his unwillingness to face the German problem directly, he adds: "And we are in complete agreement with Hitler when he proclaims that politics only achieves its superior form if it is racial."[51] He quickly adds, though, that the term racial does not refer to the physical attributes of a people, but to their moral and cultural contributions.

Giraudoux's life in his last few years was very much affected by the war. In 1939, the Daladier[52] government named him commissaire général à l'information, a position that involved creating propaganda for France as the country prepared for its forthcoming conflict. Giraudoux's publication, *Full Powers,* may have had some role in his appointment, since the work seemed to indicate that he might be suitable for the position. However, he was no administrator, and he was unable to cope with the bureaucracy. In addition, the speeches and radio addresses that he gave were too witty and too removed from the actual situation. Blunt, direct talk was needed in time of war, and Giraudoux was not the man for that. When the Daladier government was replaced, the writer was released from his position.

For a man who was slow in recognizing the dangers of Hitler, this reality came upon him rapidly. France fell to the Germans in June 1940, and Giraudoux suffered tremendously from this catastrophe. At the same time, his son, Jean-Pierre, joined the de Gaulle forces in London, and Giraudoux died before seeing him again. During the next few years, the author divided his time between Paris and the family property in Cusset, where he could be with his mother, his brother, and his brother's son (Giraudoux's godson), also named Jean Giraudoux. Cusset was very close to Vichy, where the government of Marshall Pétain had taken up residence. At the beginning, like many others, the writer was taken in by the Vichy government, and he thought that he might be able to work within it for the betterment of France. For a short time, he accepted a position as the curator of historical monuments. He also actively sought, but did not receive, a position as commissioner for urbanism in the Vichy government, a position he wanted so that he could follow through on his ideas about city life.

It is difficult to know with certainty Giraudoux's attitude toward the Germans during the war. There is no doubt that he detested the war, not only for what it was doing to his country, but for the division it caused between Germany and France, one of the major themes in his writing. With his own son working with the de Gaulle forces, and his stepson, Christian Pineau,[53] arrested and deported by the Germans, the author had ample personal reasons to abhor

what was taking place. However, at the same time, he kept up his contacts with some of the German officers in Paris, mostly those who were intellectuals or literary figures. Although there seems to have been an initial naiveté about his understanding of Germany's intentions at the beginning of the war, later Giraudoux did participate, in a limited way, in the resistance to German occupation. He apparently accumulated considerable documentation on the abuses of the Nazi troops in France, although such documentation has never been found among his papers. In addition, according to Jean Blanzat,[54] Giraudoux had written a reply to Marshall Pétain, in which he said that Frenchmen would never be willing to work in German factories during the war, but this reply has also disappeared.

What has remained is an unfinished manuscript that he was working on at the time of his death, a work meant to complement recommendations that he had previously set forth in *Full Powers*. This manuscript, *Sans pouvoirs (Without Powers),* published posthumously in 1946, was meant to be a political message for liberated France. Once again, the author was turning to a better time, a moment when France would no longer have to endure the shame of the occupation. In this respect, it is quite possible that this type of attitude was responsible for his less than full resistance during the war years. The writer never seemed able to cope with the problems of the moment — he always sought the ideal beyond the immediate reality. In this work, Giraudoux criticizes the then current French leaders, who were blaming the citizens for what had happened to France. The writer rejects these statements from his leaders, pointing out that 1,500,00 Frenchmen died in World War I and that the country was exhausted after that conflict. But, he maintains, France will not accept the word defeat and will find new confidence. In the chapter entitled "Protocol," Giraudoux condemns the leaders of the between war period. They lacked imagination and did not help the French people find their way. In "Finances," the writer claims that those in charge failed in their duties — they created a money without value, and people found themselves without enough on which to live. The financial policies created the ruin of respect for authority and the separation of the citizen from his sense of community within the state.

Returning to one of his favorite subjects, Giraudoux also underlines the importance of urbanism, that "gathering of measures by which a nation can assure itself the rhythm and the bearing of mod-

ern life.''[55] France's first mission is to preserve important historical
sites, and the second, to modernize the country and open it up to
the present century. In "Sports," he mentions the necessity of a
healthy body, another frequent topic of the author. The possibility
of achieving this healthy body must be available to all, not just to
an elite. "Education" has also been too limited to an elite and must
be widened to help remake the patterns of French living. In his
final chapter, "The Future of France," Giraudoux comments that
man brought this war upon himself by his lack of imagination. The
people with skills, technique, and imagination have not been
allowed to improve the quality of life, and this situation must be
changed. At the same time, intellectual activity must also be
allowed to flourish, and each man should be permitted to retain his
differences and his individuality.[56]

During this very depressing period of the war, with his son in
London, Giraudoux was also in effect separated from his wife, and
in the last few months of his life, when not in Cusset, he lived in the
Hôtel de Castille in Paris. His health was worsening, and he suffered from severe attacks of bronchitis during the winter. The one
aspect of life that kept him going was his writing. Besides the plays
and the articles, he was also apparently thinking of writing another
novel and of editing his memoirs.[57]

Moreover, in 1942, at the age of sixty, he suddenly turned to the
cinema, reasoning that the modern world required the use of up to
date means of transmitting one's ideas. However, he had not abandoned his belief in the power of words, and he maintained that
motion pictures were an art form that had language as its basis.[58]
Actually, as Janine Delort points out, Giraudoux's novelistic style
lends itself very well to the motion picture, and in a work like
Struggle with the Angel, certain passages recall cinematic tech-
niques.[59] As it turned out, Giraudoux worked on two film scripts —
La Duchesse de Langeais (The Duchess of Langeais, 1942), an
adaptation of a story by Honoré de Balzac; and *Les Anges du
péché (Angels of Sin,* 1944), a screenplay that he developed in collaboration with Robert Bresson and the Reverend P. Raymond
Bruckberger. The themes are those of the later period of this
writing: *The Duchess* tells of two people who love each other but
never at the same moment and of the impossibility of their love;
Angels of Sin deals with the question of purity and absolutism and
its effects upon humanity.

These diverse forms of writing in these last few years give evidence of a person going through a certain unrest and disarray. This unrest, however, also contained some optimism, a hope for the future, whether expressed in a play like *The Madwoman of Chaillot* or the manuscript on which he was working at the time of his death, *Without Powers.* In spite of the overwhelmingly crushing reality around him, in spite of his considerable pessimism, a strong feeling for life still managed to exist within Giraudoux, and even at the end, he found hope amidst the despair.

XIII   *Style: The Ultimate Triumph Over Reality*

Although reality may have eventually taken the upper hand in Giraudoux's life, he always possessed one means of triumphing over it: his style. Through style, he could create a world of the imagination and enter the realm of the poetic. Like the controller in *Intermezzo,* the writer could take what reality had to offer and bring into being a better world. Thus, he could transcend his everyday life, develop his own universe, and experience the sense of harmony that each of his protagonists sought. By establishing his own world, he could, in a sense, become the equal of a god, with all the resultant powers and authority. Giraudoux's universe is essentially one of innocence, before the fall of man, a pre-Adamite state. Since the writer looks for a realm beyond the imperfections of reality, the characters in his works move in a realm of perfection, of absolutes. Basically, there is no psychological progression or development in this sphere — his characters are simply in search of preestablished essences, and when they find them, they accept them immediately. Like Electra, they await the moment when they will "declare" themselves, the moment when they will reach the state for which they are destined.

Such a conception of the world has led two major critics to interpret Giraudoux somewhat differently. Jean-Paul Sartre sees Giraudoux's world as one of archetypes and "substantial forms," a universe in which no further development takes place in the character.[60] This domain, where man realizes his essence spontaneously, where there is no question of his changing through contacts with reality, where the only freedom is the exact realization of preestablished beings, is, according to Sartre, that of Aristotle, that of logic and the rational. What astonishes the writer of *Being and Nothingness* is that Giraudoux, a contemporary author, could accept Aristotle's domain, one that has been buried for four hundred years.

Another critic, Claude-Edmonde Magny, agrees with Sartre that
Giraudoux's creation is one of "substantial forms," but she views
this as Platonic rather than Aristotelian: "The archetypes of Giraudoux are,... like the Platonic Ideas, singular essences, each one
endowed with an individual structure, making up the principal
types of organization of the real."[61]

Whichever interpretation one accepts, both writers agree that
Giraudoux's is a realm of the singular, of the unique: "Everything
in the world of Giraudoux is raised to the superlative, as is fitting,
in a universe where there is no efficient causality, no temporal
becoming, where the only imaginable change is the realization,
each day a little more perfect in each way, of one's essence."[62] One
has the feeling of the first day of creation, a beginning, a newness,
or, to use Sartre's term, a sense of "reconquered virginities."[63] In
his writing, Giraudoux is attempting to take what reality has tarnished and to return it to its pure state. In so doing, his protagonists do not move in the same spheres as ordinary human beings,
because they have been raised to the ultimate perfection. As such,
when the writer's first novels appeared, critics had an extremely
difficult time understanding them and their first reactions stressed
what seemed to be the superficiality of the works and the supposed
préciosité.

Préciosité is a word that applies to a style of speaking and writing
that developed in France in the early part of the seventeenth century. Essentially, it was a reaction against vulgarity and coarseness
in manners, and it sometimes took the form of an overrefinement
of language, resulting in exaggerated and ridiculous expressions. To
the extent that Giraudoux, too, sought to avoid the vulgarity he
found in reality and that style was an important means of arriving
at that goal, a certain parallel exists. However, préciosité in seventeenth century France often became an affectation, a superficial
facade of elegance. In Giraudoux's case it is quite different: the
unique expressions, the unexpected juxtaposition of words, the unusual metaphors are a serious attempt to create an esthetic and
moral universe. His protests against the impurity of existence led
him to develop his own universe. As LeSage indicates, this effort
on the writer's part is a "manifestation of ... 'humanism,' the
affirmation of man's control over himself and, insofar as his attitude is concerned, over nature."[64] In this way, man becomes his
own god, he becomes as powerful as any supreme being.

The writer's use of language, particularly his use of metaphors

and symbols, helps us to enter into the special reality that he is creating. In general, his metaphor or symbol is seldom extremely vivid or colorful, but it does reveal affinities not previously recognized, and it provides subtle, incisive explanations of Giraudoux's universe. In *Electra,* the playwright employs the metaphor of the hedgehogs who, out of love, cross the road to reach the other side. Inevitably, they are crushed by the feet of the horses passing over the route at the same time. Once in a while, observes the beggar in the play, you find one who has died, "a tiny young one, who is not stretched out exactly like the others,... the small foot rigid, the jaws firmly closed, much more honorable, and one has the impression that this one did not die as a hedgehog but that he was struck down in the place of another, in your place" (*T* II, 26). The metaphor gives a vivid description of the role of Electra, more so perhaps than a straightforward accounting could have provided. Most often, the metaphors and symbols are taken from simple, ordinary moments in life, but they are endowed with a new sense of reality. In *My Friend from Limousin,* the narrator describes his meeting with Siegfried: "I told him that he looked well. I asked him if he had eaten. These questions would have been more suitable to someone who had been operated on for appendicitis rather than to a tyrant, but he was as happy to find someone to whom he could confide his quarrels with royalty as would be a village housewife who finally perceives, out there, naked on the beach, a sister soul capable of understanding her quarrels with her maid" (*OR* I, 520). Through his original and perceptive view of the universe, Giraudoux creates a new universe and surpasses reality.

What bothered some critics when Giraudoux first began writing (and still bothers some today) was the fact that the author's somewhat detached sense of humor sometimes left the impression that he was simply engaging in facile comedy. His love of puns, his verbal conceits, his fondness for clichés lend, at times, an air of superficiality or, as Lemaître notes, make the reader think of "spoofing typical of the *canular normalien*"[65] — that is, of the student of university age. Because of his discreet personality, the writer usually did not care to show the depths of his feelings, and ironic humor was a means of separation between his inner self and his reader. Until the last phase of his writing, he generally did not display his more serious side, preferring the detachment that humor allows. In so doing, he also managed to keep his universe harmonious, not permitting the pettiness of the world to upset the equilibrium of the perfection that he sought to create. The imperfections of reality might enter his domain from time to time, but the writer could lessen their impact by his witty and stylized view. Such an approach, however, also created a misunderstanding, as people found it difficult to see beyond the amusing facade that the author had created.

The early critics tried to fit Giraudoux's universe into conventional categories, but his world, basically that of the German *Märchen,* is too poetic to be placed into normal patterns. When he first began writing, his work was so different from the authors of his time that it seemed more startling than it would today when new authors have created infinite variations in style and form, both in the novel and in the theater. In a country where Balzac and Stendhal had created their own worlds, but through a generally conventional format, Giraudoux's seemingly aimless style, with its numerous digressions, created severe problems for his readers. The writer, however, saw himself as part of a special group at that time: "We wanted to react, to break the mold, to give free rein to invention. The war created this reaction in us."[66]

Spontaneity certainly seems to be one of the major bases of his method of composition, particularly of his novels. As we noted earlier, Giraudoux approached his writing often without a clear idea about the form that his narrative would take, and he would allow himself to be guided by the inspiration of the moment. "I do not feel responsible to anyone whatsoever for what I do,"[67] he observed at one point. In an interview in 1923, he indicated very clearly why he felt free to follow his own inclinations: "I consider everything I have written only as a sort of poetic wandering, and I have never had the pretention to write any kind of novel or literary composition."[68] While there may be some oversimplification in this statement, the writer is pointing out that the inspiration of the moment has more validity for him than a carefully developed structure or format. It is known that he wrote very quickly and that he could compose scenes of plays or chapters of novels in relatively short periods of time. Moreover, he never gave the impression to his friends that he was doing much work. They rarely saw him writing, and he did not speak too often about it. He apparently could — and did — write in any location, either at home or at work or in a hotel on vacation, and he was not bound by any particular schedule. Nevertheless, he succeeded in completing a substantial number of works.

In effect, *Siegfried,* Giraudoux's first play, is very much a well-structured play, with a beginning, middle, and end. However, as the dramatist began to gain more confidence in this new genre, he developed a freer, less restricted form for his theater. The inventiveness of the language, the unexpected thought process involved in the creation of dialogue, the sometimes subtle, sometimes playful Giraudoux wit established the style that was to be characteristic of the author during his theatrical career. Moreover, he began to experiment with theatrical form and took his audience into his confidence. In *Intermezzo,* the druggist speaks directly to the audience, announcing that his purpose in the comedy is to act as a buffer between the vulgar reality of the inspector's scenes and the poetic reality of the forthcoming scenes with the specter. In *Electra,* the gardener steps before the curtain to explain to the spectators what is really taking place.

In both the theatrical and novelistic genres, Giraudoux's natural tendency was toward improvisation, toward a spontaneous expression. However, almost all of his works have an overall structure that provides form for his formless world. As Laurent LeSage has pointed out,[75] rhetorical devices such as polarity, antithesis, and contrast are found at the basis of Giraudoux's writing. Antithesis, whether it be France and Germany, man and woman, the real and the ideal, or principle and compromise, gives shape to the author's universe. Each contrasting side is presented as an essence — that is, in its absolute position — and as a result, his writings tend to deal with extreme situations. Giraudoux wants us to understand his conception of reality by a comparison of opposites. When Hector and Ulysses sit down in *Tiger at the Gates* to discuss war and peace, the contrasting opinions of the two men provide a provocative and stimulating debate of the issue. Giraudoux does not attempt to resolve the problem for us — he presents the two points of view and allows us to arrive at whatever truths we can uncover. Basically, it is his hope that somehow these opposing opinions will find common grounds, that somehow a merger of the two sides will be achieved. With the exception of *Bella* and *The Madwoman of Chaillot,* it is not a question of one side being right and the other wrong, and the merits of the debate often switch from one group to the other. In effect, Giraudoux's endings are often purposely ambiguous and unclear, because they reflect a similar inability to resolve the conflicts in his personal life. We do not have to accept Sartre's opinion that Giraudoux's work makes one think of a "schizophrenic who cannot adapt himself to reality,"[76] but we can readily accept Magny's view, previously noted, that Giraudoux's writings show "the impossibility confronting us of knowing the definitive truth about anything whatsoever."[77]

Although reality may have prevented Giraudoux from resolving the conflicts in his own life, thus necessitating an ambiguity in his works, he nevertheless succeeded in finding a certain sense of perfection in the universe created by his style. Here, the writer was able to transport himself from the everyday to a better existence of his own making — at least temporarily.

CHAPTER 5

Conclusion

T HE Golden Age of Giraudoux has passed, and he no longer dominates French drama as he once did. In the 1930s, he was the major French playwright of the twentieth century, and no one else up to that time had succeeded in capturing the attention of both the critics and the public. However, with the passage of time, the writer has not retained the eminence that he once held, and other prominent dramatists have appeared. Jean Anouilh, some of whose writing is similar to Giraudoux's, has also managed to achieve the lengthy and worthy esteem of critics and public. In the 1950s, the theatrical world began to change considerably, with the arrival of the Theater of the Absurd or the *nouveau théâtre,* and such playwrights as Samuel Beckett, Eugène Ionesco, and Jean Genet imposed their theatrical visions. Suddenly, dialogue began to lose much of its importance, and in fact, language, upon which Giraudoux had built so much of his theater, was devalued, with actions speaking more directly than words. The influence of Antonin Artaud, a theoretician of the theater who died in 1947, became more pronounced, and his theories, in which words were only one part of a whole that also included sound and visual effects, had a major impact. As this trend away from the word continued (and still continues to the present day), directors began to assume greater control of the stage performance, and soon these *metteurs-en-scène* or *régisseurs* became more prominent than the dramatists.

There is no way of predicting if future theater will see a continuation along these lines or if the drama of dialogue or language will recapture some of its former importance. Giraudoux's theater, in which language and stylistic devices play such a vital role, has inevitably faded somewhat from the mainstream of attention. Yet it would be a mistake to assume that he does not still have a public. Since his death, his plays have been frequently presented, and

145

within the past few years, works like *Tiger at the Gates, The Mad-woman of Chaillot, Ondine,* and *Amphitryon 38* have been revived successfully in Paris. Moreover, in his novels, he may reach a new level of interest among the public. His numerous digressions, whimsical inventiveness, and disregard for traditional structure should seem less difficult to a public that has had to contend with an even more radical use of structure in "new" novelists like Alain Robbe-Grillet, Michel Butor, or Nathalie Sarraute. And the scholarly world has shown renewed interest in Giraudoux; eight book length studies on him have appeared since 1971, including four within the past four years.[1]

The richness and complexity of Giraudoux's work have been explored in many of these studies, which have proven that the dramatist-novelist is a writer of considerable substance. Far from being someone who has ignored reality, he has constantly had it on his mind, and in every one of his works, he has asked the one essential question: How can man best cope with reality? Each one of his works has revealed that he was struggling with an imperfect existence, hoping for the absolute, longing for perfection. In essence, the public, whether it was aware of it or not, responded to this one overriding theme of the author. Giraudoux had managed to touch a sensitive nerve, as everyone understood the need to go beyond the difficulties of daily activity, to transcend the humdrum of life. Upon entering the domain of Giraudoux, we find ourselves in a new, and hopefully better, reality. We have a sense of being transported to a different world.

As we have seen throughout the course of this study, Girau-doux's writings have a surprisingly close relationship to major pre-occupations in his own life, and they reflect the problems that the author was facing in his own reality. The conflicts of France and Germany, man and woman, purity and defilement represent his attempts to come to grips with the difficulties surrounding him in his daily life. There now seems no doubt that the author had a deeper, more sensitive, and finally, more tragic view of the universe than people had originally suspected. Yet at the same time, he was not always able to communicate the depths of his feelings, the full extent of his sense of tragedy. We have already observed that, as a schoolboy, he was detached from the people around him and expressed a certain indifference to ordinary life. Even as an adult writer, he seemed unwilling to make a direct commitment of too much of his inner being to his works, as if he were still retaining his detachment and his indifference.

Interestingly enough, Giraudoux's stylistic excellence, including his verbal inventiveness and wit, often covers up his deepest preoccupations. At the same time, paradoxically, Giraudoux himself is always present in his novels and plays, but his presence is established through his themes, debated by characters who do not exist to any great extent other than as an expression of their author's ideas. As a result, Giraudoux's concerns do not exist as a reality for us, because he has not anchored them in characters of substance; while the characters are Giraudoux's spokesmen, they do not reflect enough life to make us understand the depths of the writer's preoccupations. These preoccupations, as expressed, seem like discussions of abstract ideas rather than the very real and very troubling problems that they represented to the author.

Giraudoux was a sensitive, creative, and witty writer whose search for a better reality affected the public of his time and still retains a great appeal, even for the more complex, present-day generation. Yet his innate discretion and detachment, reflected in his novels and plays, tends to lessen the impact of these works. As a result, Giraudoux seems likely to continue to be considered a first-rate, important writer, even if he eventually falls short of being a major figure of world literature.

Notes and References

Chapter One

1. Albert Pons, "Jean Giraudoux au lycée de Châteauroux ou l'art de présider les distributions de prix," *Les Nouvelles Litteraires,* 28 July 1928, p. 5.

2. René Marill Albérès, *Esthétique et morale chez Jean Giraudoux* (Paris: Nizet, 1957), p. 17.

3. Jean-Pierre Giraudoux, *Le Fils* (Paris: Grasset, 1967), pp. 43–44.

4. Laurent LeSage, *Jean Giraudoux: His Life and Works* (University Park: The Pennsylvania State University Press, 1959), p. 12. The only two writers known to have answered were Charles-Louis Philippe and Edmond Rostand.

5. Jean Giraudoux, "Visitations," in *Oeuvres littéraires diverses* (Paris: Grasset, 1958), p. 703. All future references to material published in this work will be incorporated into the text under the abbreviation *OLD.*

6. Located in Paris, the Ecole Normale Supérieure is a center of preparation for important university positions. However, many of its graduates go on to success in other areas, such as diplomacy, politics, literature, or business.

7. Jacques Body, *Giraudoux et l'Allemagne* (Paris: Didier, 1975), p. 30.

8. Georges Lemaître, *Jean Giraudoux: The Writer and His Work* (New York: Frederick Ungar, 1971), pp. 7–8.

9. The *Licence-ès-lettres* is a university degree that, at that time, was roughly the equivalent of a Master of Arts degree in the United States.

10. Both LeSage and Albérès state that Giraudoux was working on an advanced degree in German during his first year at the école. However, the more recent work by Jacques Body (pp. 34–36). maintains that Giraudoux probably did not begin his German studies until his second year.

11. Body, p. 39.

12. *Lettres,* ed. Jacques Body (Paris: Editions Klincksieck, 1975), pp. 52–53.

13. The *Diplôme d'Etudes Supérieures* is an advanced degree between the *Licence* and the *Agrégation.*

14. The *Agrégation* is a rigorous, competitive examination for univer-

sity students that leads to placement as teachers in lycées or in some universities.

15. Albérès, p. 48.

16. These stories were published in 1952 by Gallimard under the title *Les Contes d'un matin.*

17. Another term for this period is that used by Roger Shattuck as the title of his book, *The Banquet Years, rev. ed. (New York: Vintage Books, 1968).*

18. Lemaître, p. 15.

19. The future Madame Giraudoux was divorced at the time from Colonel Paul Pineau by whom she had had two children, Christian and Arlette, the latter of whom died at a young age (Lemaître, p. 18).

20. André Bourin, "Elle et lui: Chez Madame Jean Giraudoux," *Les Nouvelles Littéraires,* 16 November 1950, p. 1.

21. Both Albérès and Body state that the marriage took place during the year 1921, but Lemaître lists the date as 1918.

22. A more detailed background on the Berthelot-Poincaré dispute will be presented in the section dealing with the novel *Bella.*

23. Body, p. 272.

24. Jean Barreyre, "*Siegfried* et Giraudoux," *Candide,* 24 May 1928, p. 13.

25. A *festschrift* is a volume of articles or essays usually written in homage to a retired professor.

26. Barreyre, p. 13.

27. J.-P. Giraudoux, p. 71.

28. Ibid., p. 84.

29. Lemaître, pp. 27–28.

30. J.-P. Giraudoux, p. 98.

31. Gilbert Ganne, "Jean-Pierre Giraudoux: Un Fils régent en exil," *Les Nouvelles Littéraires,* 18 December 1969, p. 11.

32. Body, p. 449.

Chapter Two

1. Body, pp. 138–41.

2. Ernest Theodor Amadeus Hoffmann (1766–1822) wrote tales of madness and the supernatural that made him one of the acknowledged masters of fantastic fiction.

3. Body, pp. 142–43.

4. LeSage, p. 34.

5. Albérès, p. 56.

6. *Oeuvre romanesque,* I (Paris: Grasset, 1955), 105–106. All future references to this collection will be referred to as *OR* I and incorporated into the text. In addition, all references to the second volume, also published in 1955, will be listed as *OR* II and incorporated into the text.

150 JEAN GIRAUDOUX

7. *Lectures pour une ombre* (Paris: Emile-Paul, 1917) was translated by Elizabeth S. Sergeant under the title *Campaigns and Intervals* (New York: Houghton Mifflin, 1918).

8. Albérès, p. 70.

9. Body, p. 213.

10. Jean-Marc Aucuy states that Giraudoux was not a prodigy but a hard-working pupil who strove for perfection (*La Jeunesse de Giraudoux* [Paris: Spid, 1948], pp. 78–79).

11. Lemaître (p. 57) claims that Jacques de Bolny was modeled after Maurice Bunau-Varilla, the editor of the newspaper *Le Matin,* for which Giraudoux worked at one time.

12. The previous works that he called novels (*The School for the Indifferent, Campaigns and Intervals,* and so forth) are essentially collections of short stories, essays, or diaries.

13. Albérès, p. 260.

Chapter Three

1. The *jeune fille,* in the adolescence of her life, is the perfect Giraudoux protagonist, for she possesses the imagination to allow her to act as an intermediary between the real and the unreal.

2. Suzanne, of course, accommodated herself to nature. As Philippe Berthier notes, Robinson Crusoe did exactly the opposite. He "transported Europe to the Pacific and created the marvel of totally destroying the exoticism which surrounded him" ("*Suzanne et le Pacifique* ou l'anti-Robinson Crusoé," *Revue des Sciences Humaines,* January-June 1970, p. 138).

3. Charles P. Marie, *La Réalité humaine chez Jean Giraudoux* (Paris: La Pensée Universelle, 1975), p. 9.

4. LeSage, pp. 47–48.

5. In 1923, Louis Collier Willcox translated the work under the title *My Friend from Limousin* (New York: Harper).

6. André Lang, *Tiers de siècle* (Paris: Plon, 1935), p. 218.

7. André Salmon, *Souvenirs sans fin,* 2 (Paris: Gallimard, 1956), 172–73.

8. The name "Siegfried" comes from the great folk hero of early and medieval Germanic mythology. "Von Kleist" is the German dramatic poet Heinrich von Kleist (1777–1811), whose writings Giraudoux had previously studied.

9. René Marill Albérès, *La Genèse de "Siegfried" de Jean Giraudoux* (Paris: Minard, 1963), p. 18.

10. Body (pp. 15–17) argues that, in spite of Giraudoux's attachment to Romantic Germany, in many ways he was anti-German. From his educational training as a child, he probably bore the grudges of his former

teachers, particularly regarding a problem like the Alsace-Lorraine dispute.

11. However, Giraudoux utilized many of his impressions from his trip in the work. See Body (pp. 237–46) for a detailed account of what the novelist put into his book following his visit to Germany.

12. Bourin, p. 1.

13. Body, p. 223.

14. This brief work was published separately in 1923, a year before the publication of *Juliette.*

15. Body, p. 274.

16. Giraudoux apparently only stayed in the post for five days, asking for a two month leave of absence for health reasons (Body, p, 272).

17. Albérès, *Esthétique,* p. 177.

18. This time, however, the protagonist, Bella, is a young woman of twenty-five, no longer the innocent adolescent of the previous works.

19. Lemaître, p.23.

20. Ibid., p. 73.

21. Benjamin Crémieux in particular had encouraged Giraudoux to turn the novel into a play. In addition, Giraudoux had thought of adapting the work for the cinema (Albérès, *La Genèse,* p. 29).

22. Lemaître, p. 94.

23. Albérès, *La Genèse,* p. 30.

24. Augustin Eugène Scribe (1791–1861) wrote plays that were models of tight, careful construction but that were generally lacking in artistic value. Scribe's approach to playwrighting brought about the expression, "the well-made play," the *pièce bien faite.*

25. Body, p. 294.

26. *Théâtre,* I (Paris: Grasset, 1954), 54. All future references will be abbreviated to *T* I and incorporated into the text. In addition, all references to vol. II of *Théâtre,* also published by Grasset in 1954, will be listed as *T* II.

27. The Siegfried theme was so important to Giraudoux that he could not abandon it once he had started it, continuing to publish variations on it. In 1928, he published the beginning of the third act of *Siegfried von Kleist* under the title "Divertissement de Siegfried." Later, in 1930, another revision appeared under the title *Fugues sur Siegfried.* Then, in 1935, the fourth act of *Siegfried von Kleist* was published under the title "Fin de Siegfried" (this fourth act can be found in vol. I of Giraudoux's *Théâtre*).

28. *The Impromptu of Paris* was inspired by Molière's *L'Impromptu de Versailles.* In Giraudoux's work, Jouvet and the actors in his troupe discuss the state of theater at the time. The play was first presented on December 4, 1937, as a curtain raiser to a revival of *Tiger at the Gates.* The dramatist's other comments on the theater are found in the sections 'Littérature'' and "Autour du théâtre" found in the previously cited *Oeuvres littéraires diverses.* Another important essay, "Le Théâtre contemporain

en Allemagne et en France," can be found in *Or dans le nuit* (Paris: Grasset, 1969), pp. 132–84.

29. Erwin Piscator (1893–1966) was a German theatrical director and producer who, along with Bertolt Brecht, was the foremost exponent of Epic theater.

30. Body, p. 368.

31. André Antoine's *Théâtre Libre* was an important theatrical movement at the end of the nineteenth century (1887–1894), specializing in Naturalistic drama.

32. Body, p. 308.

33. See J.-J. Anstett, "A propos d'*Amphitryon 38* — Jean Giraudoux and H. von Kleist," *Les Langues Modernes,* 42, 4A (August-September-October 1948), 385–93.

34. Body, pp. 309–10.

35. On October 9, 1934, the play was revived by Jouvet at the Théâtre de l'Athénée with a new version of the third act, which can be found in the Jouvet holdings at the Library of the Arsenal in Paris. However, the new version did not replace the original third act published in the Grasset edition (Jacques Robichez, *Le Théâtre de Giraudoux* [Paris: SEDEC, 1976], p. 28).

36. Charles Mauron, *Le Théâtre de Giraudoux* (Paris: José Corti, 1971), p. 83.

37. *Amphitryon 38,* ed. Pierre Brunel (Paris: Bordas, 1970), p. 115.

38. Pierre Marivaux (1688–1763), French dramatist and novelist, was best known for the grace and style of his love comedies.

39. Claude-Edmonde Magny, *Précieux Giraudoux* (Paris: Editions du Seuil, 1945), p. 103.

40. Roy Lewis, "Giraudoux's Dark Night of the Soul: A Study of *Les Aventures de Jérôme Bardini*," *French Studies,* 28, no. 4 (October 1974), 421.

41. Albérès (*Esthétique,* p. 321) states that the name of "The Kid" comes from the Charlie Chaplin film.

42. Ibid., p. 324.

43. Ibid., pp. 497–98.

44. Body (p. 335) feels that Giraudoux probably was more acquainted with Hebbel's version of *Judith* than with Bernstein's. In addition, Hebbel's version is found on the list drawn up by Giraudoux.

45. Lemaître, p. 105.

46. Body, p. 332. Body also maintains that Giraudoux displayed a certain anti-Semitism: "Giraudoux was never a declared anti-Semite, but, in spite of himself, he breathed the germs of a certain racist propaganda, which was virulent in France and in Germany at the time of his youth, and of which his work bears traces which are reduced but nonetheless unpleasant" (p. 329).

47. As Yves Moraud points out: "She kills Holofernes so that she can

possess forever the man who possessed her" (*"Judith" ou l'impossible liberté* [Paris: Lettres Modernes, No. 125, 1971], p. 55).

48. Lemaître, p. 110.

49. Claude Roy, "Giraudoux et les Dieux," *Cahiers Madeleine Renaud — Jean-Louis Barrault,* No. 36 (November 1961), p. 30.

50. Moraud, p. 60.

51. Will L. McLendon, "A Compositional Aspect of Giraudoux's Novels: The 'Offshoot' Chapters," *Orbis Litterarum*, 23 (1968), 233–46.

52. Ibid., p. 241.

53. The *commedia dell'arte* was a popular form of comedy employing improvised dialogues and masked characters that flourished in Italy from the sixteenth to the eighteenth centuries. Both Body and Colette Weil feel that Giraudoux was not serious when he stated that the *commedia dell'arte* was the main source of *Intermezzo*. See Body (p. 348), and Weil (*Intermezzo, Edition critique* [Paris: Editions Ophrys, 1975], p. 44).

54. See Body, pp. 347–52, and Weil, pp. 37–42.

55. Body, pp. 350–52.

56. Weil (pp. 39–40) points out that the title may have come from Heinrich Heine's *Intermezzo,* written in 1823. Giraudoux had claimed that his *Intermezzo* was an interlude between two tragedies, *Judith* and *Brutus* (the latter play never appeared). This statement closely parallels one made by Charles Andler in one of his courses on German literature when he noted that Heine's *Intermezzo* was a lyrical interlude between two tragedies.

57. Whether the ghost is alive at the beginning of the play or not is open to question. Louis Jouvet felt that the specter was a part of the spirit world right from the start of the play. Colette Weil suggests that the ghost may be an aspect of Isabelle's soul: "In that case, she [Isabelle] would be carrying on a discussion with herself and the play would be an allegory" (p. 35).

58. Judith shares some of the qualities of the *jeune fille,* but her destiny is so much more tragic that she cannot be classified with the other young girls like Suzanne and Isabelle.

59. Janine Delort, "A propos d'une adaptation: *Tessa* de Jean Giraudoux," *Annales Publiées par la Faculté des Lettres et des Sciences Humaines de Toulouse — Caliban VII,* 6, fasc. 1 (1970), 43.

60. Ibid., p. 49.

61. See J.-P. Giraudoux.

62. Briand was also the chief architect of the Locarno Pact (1925) and the Kellogg-Briand Pact (1926), which were designed to establish European security and to create peace. In 1926, he was given the Nobel Peace Prize.

Chapter Four

1. The literal translation of the title is *The Trojan War Will Not Take*

Place. However, *Tiger at the Gates* is the title used in the English translation by Christopher Fry (New York: Oxford University Press, 1956).

2. Giraudoux claimed in an interview that he did not intend to write a work of actuality (Benjamin Crémieux, "M. Jean Giraudoux et 'La Guerre de Troie n'aura pas lieu,' " *Je Suis Partout,* No. 263 [7 December 1935], p. 4).

3. There are many possible sources for the play. Albérès (*Esthétique,* p. 396) sees Tolstoy's *War and Peace* as a major influence. Body (pp. 364–66) again refers to Goethe, and Mary Maclean sees a connection between Giraudoux and Frank Wedekind ("Jean Giraudoux and Frank Wedekind," *Australian Journal of French Studies,* 4, no. 1 [January-April 1967], 102).

4. Body, p. 370.

5. Crémieux, p. 4.

6. Captain James Cook (1728–1779) was an English naval captain and explorer who set sail in the "Endeavour" to the South Seas, including Tahiti. He wrote an account of his trip, covering the years 1769–1771.

7. Giraudoux took the last name for the character from a Joseph Banks (1743–1820), who was Cook's naturalist on his trip.

8. *La Menteuse* (Paris: Grasset, 1969), p. 277.

9. Ibid., p. 269.

10. Lemaître, p. 83.

11. Body, p. 376.

12. Ibid., p. 376.

13. Lise Gauvin, *Giraudoux et le thème d'Electre,* No. 108 (Paris: Lettres Modernes, 1969), p. 38.

14. The imminent war between France and Germany, which had been a source of great distress to him, seemed to preoccupy him less for the moment. There is even reason to believe that Giraudoux did not fully grasp the dangers of Hitler's rise to power (see Body, pp. 385–89).

15. A. Warnod, "J'ai épousseté le buste d'Electre, nous dit M. Jean Giraudoux," *Le Figaro,* 11 May 1937, p. 3.

16. Another play, Sophocles' *Antigone,* may also have had a special influence (Gauvin, pp. 28, 36).

17. *Electre,* ed. Michelle Brier (Paris: Bordas, 1972), p. 120.

18. *Electre,* ed. Brier, p. 121.

19. Bourin, p. 1.

20. Lemaître, pp. 88–89. See also Madame Giraudoux's comments in Bourin, p. 1.

21. See Lemaître, pp. 89–90.

22. Madeleine Ozeray, "Tout n'est que signe," in *Cahiers Jean Giraudoux — "Ondine,"* 2–3 (Paris: Grasset, 1973–1974), 35–39.

23. La Motte-Fouqué (1777–1843) was a German poet and novelist who wrote many chivalric romances, novels, plays, and epics.

24. Body (p. 392) lists the date as 1907, and Monique Brosse ("Person-

nages et situations mythiques dans l''Ondine' de Giraudoux,'*Rivista di letterature moderne e comparate,* [22 September 1969], p. 183), states that it was 1906. The program notes for the first presentation of the play indicate that Giraudoux began writing the essay in 1909.

25. Laurent LeSage, " 'Die Einheit von Fouques *Undine,*' an unpublished essay in German by Jean Giraudoux," *Romanic Review,* 42 (1951), 122–34.

26. Body, p. 396.

27. Lise Gauvin "Le Théâtre dans le théâtre ou le spectacle sans illusion," in *Cahiers Jean Giraudoux — "Ondine,"* p. 75.

28. J.-P. Giraudoux, p. 86.

29. Body, pp. 399–400.

30. Wolfgang G. Sohlich, "Giraudoux's *Ondine:* The Shape of Ambiguity," *Romanistisches Jahrbuch,* 24 (1973), 137.

31. Ibid., p. 132.

32. Body, p. 403.

33. Ibid., pp. 405–406.

34. Ibid., p. 440, n. 24.

35. Bourin, p. 1.

36. Albérès, *Esthétique,* pp. 448–54.

37. Donald Inskip, *Jean Giraudoux: The Making of a Dramatist* (London: Oxford University Press, 1958), p. 149.

38. At this first presentation in Paris, Jouvet combined the short play with Jean Genet's then shocking one act work, *Les Bonnes (The Maids),* a most curious combination.

39. See Lemaître, p. 142, and Robichez, p. 45.

40. Agnès Raymond, *Jean Giraudoux: The Theory of Victory and Defeat* (Amherst: University of Massachusetts Press, 1966), p. 149.

41. See Robert Cohen, *Giraudoux: Three Faces of Destiny* (Chicago: The University of Chicago Press, 1968), pp. 116–29; and Raymond, pp. 125–53.

42. Body, p. 449.

43. Christopher Fry translated the play into English under the title of *Duel of Angels* (London: Methuen, 1958).

44. LeSage, *Jean Giraudoux,* p. 80.

45. Inskip, p. 162.

46. Jean-Louis Barrault, "Jean Giraudoux et 'Pour Lucrèce,' " *Cahiers Madeleine Renaud — Jean-Louis Barrault,* No. 2 (1953), p. 72.

47. The Université des Annales was a "private institution catering mostly to cultured society men and more particularly to society women" (Lemaître, p. 30).

48. The work was published in 1951 by Gallimard.

49. Body, p. 374.

50. *Pleins Pouvoirs* (Paris: Gallimard, 1939), p. 62.

51. Ibid., p. 76.

52. Edouard Daladier (1884–1970) was premier of France several times over the course of the years. As premier, he signed the Munich Pact, which has since become a symbol of appeasement to the Germans.

53. Pineau was Madame Giraudoux's son by her first marriage. He has served as a minister in several postwar governments in France.

54. Jean Blanzat, "Giraudoux et la Résistance," *Le Figaro,* 23 Sept. 1944, p. 2.

55. *Sans pouvoirs* (Monaco: Editions du Rocher, 1946), p. 93.

56. Giraudoux also worked on another series of texts dealing with urban problems, most of which were published in newspapers or journals during the late 1930s. This series of articles was published in 1947 by Editions Arts et Métiers Graphiques under the title, *Pour une politique urbaine (In Consideration of an Urban Politics).*

57. *Souvenir de deux existences* (Paris: Grasset, 1975) is probably the memoir on which he was working. The book contains short accounts of Giraudoux's earlier life, written by the author between 1941 and 1943.

58. Janine Delort, "La Dernière 'Tentation' de Giraudoux: cinéma," *Littérature XVII — Annales Publiées par la Faculté des Lettres et Sciences Humaines de Toulouse,* 6, fasc. 2 (1970), 78. Delort also reports, however, that Giraudoux never changed his opinion that the theater was a living spectacle whereas the cinema was a dead spectacle.

59. Ibid., p. 85.

60. Jean-Paul Sartre, "M. Jean Giraudoux et la philosophie d'Aristote à propos des 'Choix des élues,' " in *Situations I* (Paris: Gallimard, 1947), pp. 76–91.

61. Magny, p. 31.

62. Ibid., p. 21.

63. Sartre, p. 83.

64. LeSage, *Jean Giraudoux,* p. 192.

65. Lemaître, p. 194.

66. Simone Ratel, "Entretien avec M. Jean Giraudoux," *Comoedia,* 18 July 1928, p. 1.

67. George Charensol, "Comment écrivez-vous? — Jean Giraudoux," *Les Nouvelles Littéraires,* 19 December 1931, p. 8.

68. Frédéric Lefèvre, "Une Heure avec M. Jean Giraudoux," *Les Nouvelles Littéraires,* 2 June 1923, p. 1.

69. Luc Decaunes, "En relisant 'Bella' ou Jean Giraudoux romancier," *Marginales,* No. 98 (November 1964), p. 4.

70. McLendon, p. 242.

71. Decaunes, p. 8. In the seventeenth century, a number of writers described the customs of their times and were called "moralists." Jean de la Bruyère (1645–1696) was one of these moralists, and in *Caractères* (1688), he presented a number of incisive portraits of people of his period.

72. Some of these variant readings have been published in the Ides et Calendes edition of the works of Giraudoux, *Théâtre complet* (Neuchâtel

and Paris, 1945-1953), in vols. 12-15.

73. See Albérès's study, *La Genèse;* and Weil's critical edition of *Intermezzo.* Weil feels, however, that Giraudoux did not make too many changes for the improvement of dramatic construction (p. 31).

74. Albérès, *La Genèse,* p. 15.

75. LeSage, *Jean Giraudoux,* pp. 167-98.

76. Sartre, p. 76.

77. Magny, p. 103.

Chapter Five

1. The works include the previously cited books by Lemaître (1971), Mauron (1971), Body (1975), Marie (1975), Weil (1975), and Robichez (1976), as well as studies by Paul Mankin (*Precious Irony: Le Théâtre de Jean Giraudoux* [The Hague: Mouton, 1971] and by Jean-Claude Sertelon (*Giraudoux et le moyen âge* [Paris: La Pensée Universelle, 1974]).

Selected Bibliography

The list of primary sources contains the basic works written by Giraudoux. The list of secondary sources includes those works that were of special help in the preparation of this particular study. In both cases, for a complete listing, please refer to the following bibliographies:

1. Laurent LeSage, *L'Oeuvre de Jean Giraudoux. Essai de bibliographie chronologique.* Paris: Nizet; and University Park: Pennsylvania State University Press, 1956.
2. Jacques Body and Brett Dawson. *Supplément* [to the LeSage bibliography]. Bellac: Société des Amis de Jean Giraudoux, 1974.

PRIMARY SOURCES

A listing of Giraudoux's works in order of first published editions.

1. Novels, Plays, Essays

Provinciales. Paris: Grasset, 1909.
L'Ecole des indifférents. Paris: Grasset, 1911.
Lectures pour une ombre. Paris: Emile-Paul, 1917.
Simon le pathétique. Paris: Grasset, 1918.
Amica America. Paris: Emile-Paul, 1919.
Elpénor. Paris: Emile-Paul, 1919.
Adorable Clio. Paris: Emile-Paul, 1920.
Suzanne et le Pacifique. Paris: Emile-Paul, 1921.
Siegfried et le Limousin. Paris: Grasset, 1922.
Juliette au pays des hommes. Paris: Emile-Paul, 1924.
Bella. Paris: Grasset, 1926.
Eglantine. Paris: Grasset, 1927.
Siegfried. Paris: Grasset, 1928.
Amphitryon 38. Paris: Grasset, 1929.
Aventures de Jérôme Bardini. Paris: Emile-Paul, 1930.
Judith. Paris: Emile-Paul, 1931.
La France sentimentale. Paris: Grasset, 1932.
Intermezzo. Paris: Grasset, 1933.
Combat avec l'ange. Paris: Grasset, 1934.
Tessa. Paris: Grasset, 1934.

159

La Guerre de Troie n'aura pas lieu. Paris: Grasset, 1935.
Supplément au voyage de Cook. Paris: Grasset, 1937.
Electre. Paris: Grasset, 1937.
L'Impromptu de Paris. Paris: Grasset, 1937.
Les Cinq Tentations de la Fontaine. Paris: Grasset, 1938.
Cantique des cantiques. Paris: Grasset, 1939.
Choix des élues. Paris: Grasset, 1939.
Ondine. Paris: Grasset, 1939.
Pleins Pouvoirs. Paris: Gallimard, 1939.
Littérature. Paris: Grasset, 1941.
La Duchesse de Langeais. Paris: Grasset, 1942.
Sodome et Gomorrhe. Paris: Grasset, 1943.
Les Anges du péché. Paris: Gallimard, 1944.
La Folle de Chaillot. Neuchâtel and Paris: Ides et Calendes, 1945.
Sans pouvoirs. Monaco: Editions du Rocher, 1946.
L'Apollon de Bellac. Neuchâtel and Paris: Ides et Calendes, 1946.
Visitations. Neuchâtel and Paris: Ides et Calendes, 1947.
Pour une politique urbaine. Paris: Editions Arts et Métiers Graphiques,
    1947.
De Pleins Pouvoirs à Sans pouvoirs. Paris: Gallimard, 1950.
La Française et la France. Paris: Gallimard, 1951.
Les Contes d'un matin. Paris: Gallimard, 1952.
Pour Lucrèce. Paris: Grasset, 1953.
La Menteuse. Paris: Grasset, partial text, 1958; complete text, 1969.
Les Gracques. Paris: Grasset, 1958.
Portugal and Combat avec l'image. Paris: Grasset, 1958.
Or dans la nuit. Paris: Grasset, 1969.
Carnet des Dardanelles. Paris: Le Bélier, 1969.
Lettres. Paris: Editions Klincksieck, 1975.
Souvenir de deux existences. Paris: Grasset, 1975.

2. Special Editions

Théâtre complet. Neuchâtel and Paris: Ides et Calendes, 1945–1953. 16
    vols.
Théâtre. Paris: Grasset, 1954. 2 vols.
Oeuvre romanesque. Paris: Grasset, 1955. 2 vols.
Oeuvres littéraires diverses. Paris: Grasset, 1958.
Théâtre. Paris: Grasset, vol. 1 — 1958; vols. 2–4, 1959.
Théâtre. Paris: Grasset, 1971. 2 vols.

3. English Adaptations or Translations of Giraudoux's Work

Amphitryon 38. Adapted by Samuel N. Behrman. New York: Random
    House, 1938.
———. Trans. Phyllis La Farge with Peter Judd, New York: Hill & Wang,
    1964.

_____. Trans. Roger Gellert. New York: Oxford University Press, 1967.

The Apollo of Bellac (L'Apollon de Bellac). Adapted by Maurice Valency, New York: Samuel French, 1954.

_____. Abridged version. Trans. Ronald Duncan. London: Samuel French, 1957.

Bella. Trans. J. F. Scanlan. New York: Knopf, 1927.

Campaigns and Intervals (Lectures pour une ombre). Trans. Elizabeth S. Sergeant. New York: Houghton Mifflin, 1918.

Duel of Angels (Pour Lucrèce). Trans. Christopher Fry. London: Methuen, 1958.

Electra (Electre). Trans. Winifred Smith. In Eric Bentley, *From the Modern Repertoire*, Series II. Bloomington: Indiana University Press, 1952.

_____. Trans. Phyllis La Farge with Peter Judd. New York: Hill & Wang, 1964.

Elpénor. Trans. Richard Howard with Renaud Bruce. New York: Noonday Press, 1958.

Intermezzo. Adapted by Maurice Valency as *The Enchanted,* New York: Random House, 1950.

York: Oxford University Press, 1967.

_____. Trans. Roger Gellert as *Intermezzo,* New York: Oxford University Press, 1967.

Judith. Trans. John K. Savacool in Eric Bentley, *The Modern Theatre,* Vol. 3, New York: Doubleday, 1955.

_____. Trans. Christopher Fry. London: Methuen, 1963.

Lying Woman (La Menteuse). Trans. Richard Howard. New York: Winter House, 1972.

The Madwoman of Chaillot (La Folle de Chaillot). Adapted by Maurice Valency. New York: Random House, 1947.

My Friend from Limousin (Siegfried et le Limousin). Trans. Louis Collier Willcox. New York: Harper, 1923.

Ondine. Adapted by Maurice Valency. New York: Random House, 1954.

_____. Trans. Roger Gellert. New York: Oxford University Press, 1967.

Siegfried. Trans. Philip Carr. New York: L. MacVeagh-The Dial Press, 1930.

_____. Trans. Phyllis La Farge with Peter Judd. New York: Hill & Wang, 1964.

Suzanne and the Pacific (Suzanne et le Pacifique). Trans. Ben Ray Redman. New York: Putnam's Sons, 1923.

Tiger at the Gates (La Guerre de Troie n'aura pas lieu). Trans. Christopher Fry. New York: Oxford University Press, 1956.

The Virtuous Island (Supplément au Voyage de Cook). Adapted by Maurice Valency. New York: Samuel French, 1956.

SECONDARY SOURCES

1. Books

ALBÉRÈS, RENE MARILL. *Esthétique et morale chez Jean Giraudoux.* Paris: Nizet, 1957. A study long considered one o the basic works on Giraudoux. An exceptionally fine analysis of the writer's cosmic vision.

————. *La Genèse de "Siegfried" de Jean Giraudoux.* Paris: Minard, 1963. An analysis of the differences between the novel, *Siegfried et le Limousin,* and the play, *Siegfried,* explaining a great deal about Giraudoux's methods of composition.

BODY, JACQUES. *Giraudoux et l'Allemagne.* Paris: Didier, 1975. An extraordinarily fine work, tracing the influence of Germany on Giraudoux. Extremely detailed and incisive.

CAHIERS JEAN GIRAUDOUX. Paris: Grasset, vol. 1, 1973; vols. 2-3 (*Ondine*), 1973-1974; vol. 4 (*Intermezzo*), 1975. A fine series of articles about the writer and his theater.

GAUVIN, LISE. *Giraudoux et le thème d'Electre.* No. 108. Paris: Lettres Modernes, 1969. An excellent analysis of *Electre,* providing a deeper understanding of Giraudoux and his world.

GIRAUDOUX, JEAN-PIERRE. *Le Fils.* Paris: Grasset, 1967. Jean-Pierre Giraudoux's account of his father. Contains fresh insights into Giraudoux the man.

INSKIP, DONALD. *Jean Giraudoux: The Making of a Dramatist.* London: Oxford University Press, 1958. One of the first studies in English on the writer.

LEMAÎTRE, GEORGES. *Jean Giraudoux: The Writer and his Work.* New York: Frederick Ungar, 1971. A solid, thorough presentation of Giraudoux and his writings. Good, penetrating analyses of each work.

LESAGE, LAURENT. *Jean Giraudoux: His Life and Works.* University Park: Pennsylvania State University Press, 1959. Another early, basic study of Giraudoux. Especially good for its discussion of the writer's technique and style.

————. *Jean Giraudoux, Surrealism, and the German Romantic Ideal.* Urbana: University of Illinois Press, 1952. An interesting assessment of Giraudoux's relationship to the German Romantic authors.

MAGNY, CLAUDE-EDMONDE. *Précieux Giraudoux.* Paris: Editions du Seuil, 1945. An early evaluation of Giraudoux's *préciosité,* still of considerable value.

MAURON, CHARLES. *Le Théâtre de Giraudoux.* Paris: José Corti, 1971. A recent study analyzing Giraudoux from a psychocritical method.

RAYMOND, AGNES G. *Jean Giraudoux: The Theatre of Victory and Defeat.* Amherst: University of Massachusetts Press, 1966. Worthy attempt to relate Giraudoux's theater to urban and political matters.

ROBICHEZ, JACQUES. *Le Théâtre de Giraudoux.* Paris: SEDES, 1976. A particularly good study of the playwright's method of composition.

WEIL, COLETTE. *Jean Giraudoux: 'Intermezzo' (Édition critique).* Paris: Ophrys, 1975. A first-rate study of the genesis of the play, with many insights into Giraudoux the artist and creator.

2. Articles

BOURIN, ANDRE. "Elle et lui: Chez Madame Jean Giraudoux" *Les Nouvelles Littéraires,* 16 November 1950, p. 1. An interview with Madame Giraudoux, providing a number of interesting comments on Giraudoux and his relationship with his wife.

BROSSE, MONIQUE. "Personnages et situations mythiques dans l''Ondine' de Giraudoux," *Rivista di letterature moderne e comparate,* 22, fasc. 3 (September 1969), 181–203. A study of *Ondine* containing perceptive comments on Giraudoux's theater.

DECAUNES, LUC. "En relisant 'Bella' ou Jean Giraudoux romancier," *Marginales,* 98 (November 1964), 1–10. Another article dealing with a particular Giraudoux work, but including many worthwhile, general remarks on the writer's style.

MCLENDON, WILL L. "A Compositional Aspect of Giraudoux's Novels: The 'Offshoot' Chapter," *Orbis Litterarum,* 23 (1968), 233–46. A fine analysis of Giraudoux's methods in writing novels.

SARTRE, JEAN-PAUL. "M. Jean Giraudoux et la philosophie d'Aristote à propos des 'Choix des élues.' " In *Situations I,* (pp. 76–91). Paris: Gallimard, 1947. Sartre's famous study of Giraudoux's Aristotelianism.

SOHLICH, WOLFGANG G. "Giraudoux's *Ondine:* The Shape of Ambiguity," *Romanistisches Jahrbuch,* 24 (1973), 128–40. A perceptive analysis of Giraudoux's sense of theater.

Index

164